Locomotive Recognition
CLASS 37s

David N. Clough
& D. I. Rapson

CW00550852

LONDON

IAN ALLAN LTD

Contents

First published 1991

ISBN 0 7110 1919 3

Published by Ian Allan Ltd, Shepperton, Surrey; and
printed by Ian Allan Printing Ltd at their works at
Coombelands in Runnymede, England

Front cover:
No 37059 *Port of Tilbury* is seen here attaching additional vans to 7N40, the 13.27 Tyne
Yard to Tees Yard service at Tyneside CFD, Gateshead, on 15 February 1989.
Peter J. Robinson

Back cover:
Sutton Bridge Junction on 15 April 1989 plays host to No 37429 *Eisteddfod
Genedlaethol* as it heads the 07.14 Aberystwyth-London Euston off the Cambrian line.
W. A. Sharman

Preface

Class 37 has, seemingly, been a popular class since enthusiasts' attention moved from steam to diesel traction. Their following has certainly grown during the 1980s as other classes have been withdrawn. The advent of sectorisation, with its clearly defined subgroupings of locomotives, has helped identify what the 37s do, and the variations in livery associated with the way the railways are now organised provides much to study.

This is not the first book to deal with the subject. With this in mind, the authors have looked at a number of areas of study and devoted a chapter to each. Chapter 1 describes the sphere of operations on which the fleet has been deployed since 1960 in a more comprehensive way than before and is based on a considerable amount of research. The most important event in the 37s' history was the decision to undertake a life extension programme and this is covered in Chapter 2. Following from this is a description of the Class 37/0 project, showing how it fits into BR's traction policy.

Liveries can best be covered by pictorial example and this treatment is adopted for Chapter 4. It has not been practical to include every variation in paint scheme in which the type has ever appeared: only the major variants are shown. Chapter 5 sets out the strengths and weaknesses of the design in passenger service, looking also at how refurbishment has changed the performance profile. This is supplemented in Chapter 7 by description of two footplate runs on freight services. The aim here is twofold; firstly, to show how well these locomotives do moving heavy loads, and secondly, to give an insight into freight train operation. Neither of these aspects are normally available to the enthusiast.

It was sensible to look at the current allocation, both by depot and sector, to guide the reader through this field. Looked at in this way, the pattern of working falls easily into place. Finally, in keeping with the theme of the series, there are various statistics and a look at some of the 'personalities' among the class. In the latter case, three machines have been selected and the major events in their lives described. The appendices feature a definitive schedule of particulars, using official material, which should satisfy even the most inquisitive technocrat! Mike Hunt has supplied this from his extensive archive. An allocation history has been compiled by Geoff Hurst from source material. The authors are grateful to both these people for their contributions. Making a selection of photographs from the vast array available has not been easy. The intention has been to strike a balance, so providing sensible coverage of the types of work and locations in which Class 37 has appeared. It is not comprehensive; with such a large and long-lived type it could not hope to be.

The authors' aim is to inform and entertain; the objective is to offer something for all kinds of reader, whether seeking casual entertainment or detailed information.

Chapter 1

History of Workings

Following its completion at the English Electric Vulcan Works at Newton-le-Willows, the first EE Type 3 diesel, D6700, ran to Doncaster Works for acceptance trials on 2 December 1960. Trial running on the East Coast main line south of Doncaster followed, along with static tests at the Plant, and by early January 1961 D6701 and D6702 had also begun commissioning procedures. Early teething troubles included the discovery of bogie frame cracks, which necessitated a return to Vulcan Foundry for attention.

The first 30 locomotives were allocated to the Eastern Region, being based at Stratford, March, Norwich and Ipswich, and once train crew familiarisation was completed, the Type 3s began to find regular employment on passenger services out of Liverpool Street station. With the summer 1961 timetable came an acceleration of London-Norwich services, involving 16 EE Type 3 diagrams. Perhaps this was over-optimistic as only 18 of the class had been delivered at that time, and several were occupied in deputising for EE Type 4 and Brush Type 2 locomotives.

Delivery of the Great Eastern batch (D6700-D6729) was completed in October 1961, by which time the first of an allocation for the North Eastern Region was ready to take to the rails. D6730 was allocated to Hull (Dairycoates) and training trips to Scarborough, via Bridlington, began on 3 November 1961.

By the end of 1961, 32 locomotives had been delivered, and D6701/6 had received heavy repair at Stratford Works, including a power unit change for the former. On 22 December 1961, D6718 came to grief at Walthamstow (Hoe Street), becoming derailed across the passenger lines whilst shunting the 4.15am parcels from Liverpool Street. Assistance was rendered by Type 4 No D208, then the first of the class to visit the Chingford branch.

Two Type 3s visited the Midlands on 6 January 1962 when D6706 and D6712 headed football specials conveying Tottenham Hotspur supporters to Birmingham, each excursion terminating at New Street station.

Though still in the paint shop at Doncaster Works during the last few days of March 1962, D6733 was noted at Leeds on 7 April at the head of a parcels train from Hull. Delivery of the class had slowed during the winter months, and D6732/3 were not allocated to Dairycoates until the spring. Thereafter, the batch (D6730-D6741) was rapidly completed and the latter was 'on the books' at 50B by June 1962. Initially, D6730/1/2 found themselves on a variety of goods and passenger work between Hull and Doncaster, notably being employed on the up 'Yorkshire Pullman' as far as Doncaster, returning with the Hull portion of the 10.20am from King's Cross, the 5.17pm Hull-King's Cross (to Doncaster) and back home with the down Pullman.

Under the Eastern Region codes of diesel locomotive classification, the EE Type 3s were originally D17/1, until becoming D17/3 when the codes were revised from 5 March 1962. The suffix digit indicated the locomotive builders (ie figure '3' represented English Electric).

Summer Saturdays in 1962 witnessed the Type 3s hauling the hourly Clacton services over the Great Eastern, although relief and intermediate trains were operated by electric multiple-units. At the same time, the first locomotives of an eventual batch of 13 (D6742-D6754) were sent new to Sheffield Darnall depot, D6742 arriving in June 1962. The Darnall engines were soon to break new ground for the class. On 4 August 1962, D6743 was utilised on the 7.05am Sheffield to King's Cross and 3.15pm return throughout. Soon they became a common sight at King's Cross at the head of the 'Master Cutler' Pullman train from Sheffield, a most prestigious duty, until being usurped by larger diesel locomotives in 1964.

The daily 5.55pm Sheffield Victoria to Leicester Central passenger service was taken over from Brush Type 2s and on 23 July 1962 D6744 was recorded on the return leg of this particular diagram, the 10.46pm parcels from Swindon, to which the Type 3 was attached at Leicester. Such trains were routed over former Great Central metals via Loughborough, Nottingham and Staveley.

Top:
The first deliveries of D6700s were to the Great Eastern section of the Eastern Region, where they displaced EE Type 4s on the London to Ipswich, Norwich, Great Yarmouth and Lowestoft runs. This 1961 shot shows a nearly-new D6717 preparing to depart Lowestoft with a Liverpool Street train. Note the all-over green livery.   *S. Creer*

Centre:
Two decades later, Class 37 was still in charge of the Lowestoft Class 1 duties. 12 May 1984 marked the end of through locomotive-hauled passenger services from London. The honour of taking the final working went to No 37115, seen at East Suffolk Junction, Ipswich, with the 17.00 down, complete with headboard.   *M. J. Collins*

Above:
No 37266 calls at Diss on 14 June 1981 with the 08.30 Liverpool Street to Norwich.
D. M. Dawber

On 22 July 1962, D6769 was reported as being outside the paint shop at Doncaster Works. This locomotive was the first of the class to be constructed at the Darlington premises of Robert Stephenson & Hawthorn Ltd out of a total of 67 to be so delivered. As expected, D6769 was the first of the class to be allocated to Thornaby depot, although D6735/6 had been loaned there previously for crew training. By the end of the year, Thornaby had accrued 24 such locomotives for freight working in the busy Teesside area.

Following the discovery of further defects requiring repair or changing of bogies, Doncaster Works played host to two dozen of the class during the late summer months, outshopping D6700-3/5/6/8-11/3/4/5/8/20/1/3/5/7/8/9 in August 1962 and D6704/7/26 the following month.

As 1962 wore on, rarely a week went by without an EE Type 3 locomotive visiting a new location or route. Thankfully, under the expert eye of the nation's railway devotees and the associated press, much has been recorded for posterity. At the beginning of the summer timetable (18 June 1962), Type 3s replaced Brush Type 2 diesels on the Liverpool Street-Cambridge-King's Lynn express trains, with a welcome improvement in timekeeping being reported.

On 25 August 1962, D6731 (50B) worked a Hull to Southport excursion via the Calder Valley main line, and another Northwest resort, Blackpool, received its first reported Type 3 on 9 September 1962 in the shape of D6740, heading an excursion from Goole. Perhaps the most noteworthy venture was that of D6758 which was employed on a passenger working from Newcastle to Edinburgh on 19 December 1962, returning with the 2.25pm Edinburgh-Newcastle service. This was the debut of the type north of the border and, for good measure, D6758 repeated the trip the following day!

Darnall's D6742 and D6743 were sent on loan to Cardiff Canton during the autumn of 1962; later, the class became almost synonymous with South Wales. During the first week of November, D6754 was engaged on timing and oscillation trials from Doncaster Decoy Yard hauling a dynamometer car and train composed of minfits (with automatic couplers) and loaded coal wagons. The convoy ran to New England South (Peterborough) and, the following morning, to King's Cross Goods.

At the turn of the year, 93 of the class had been delivered. D6782, which had been received out of sequence, worked its acceptance trials from Doncaster during the second week of January 1963, despite having been officially allocated to Hull since November 1962.

Another test train was run on 23 January 1963, this time between Crofton (near Wakefield) and Rose Grove (Burnley) hauled by D6737. Utilising a brake tender, the

Below:
As well as taking over the London to Ipswich and beyond services, the EE Type 3s were also put to work on the King's Lynn route. A typical GE pattern signalbox controls the passage of No 37110 through Ely with the 12.36 Liverpool Street to King's Lynn on 10 June 1975. *S. Creer*

Top:
Stratford-based examples were used for many years on the Harwich boat train to Manchester, being the only daily workings by the class to the Northwest for many years. This train was routed via Woodhead until that route lost its passenger services in 1970; the Hope Valley line was used subsequently. No 37110 climbs the 1 in 10 to Cowburn Tunnel on 27 August 1976. *L. A. Nixon*

Above:
A variety of duties were allocated to the Stratford fleet. This included parcels traffic and this picture shows No 37028 passing Romford on 20 May 1977. *Kevin Lane*

Type 3 hauled 35 wagons over this steeply-graded route via Copy Pit (1 in 65/70) in the depths of an arctic winter. Three days previously, Huddersfield saw its first Type 3 in the form of D6783 which was provided to work the 9.48am (SuO) from York through to Manchester.

That same winter, two more Type 3 diagrams over the Great Central were instituted; the 3.30pm fish train from Hull to Plymouth (reporting number 3V05) and the similar 5.50pm service Hull to Banbury (3V07). Within the first few weeks, eight different class members were observed. The last of the initial Robert Stephenson & Hawthorn batch of locomotives, D6795, entered traffic in March 1963 (at Gateshead) and when D6818 was received (at Darnall) a week or so later from Vulcan Foundry, the Eastern Region's initial order for 119 machines was complete.

Following the trials with D6742/3, the Western Region received its first EE Type 3s in April 1963, at which time D6742/3 were transferred back to Sheffield. On 7 April, D6819/20/31/2/3 were all to be found in the paint shop at Doncaster Works en route to South Wales from Darlington (D6819/20) and Newton-le-Willows (D6831/2/3). An immaculate D6829 was seen at Gloucester on 4 April and Swindon shed on 29 April. Once at Cardiff, freight working commenced from Radyr Yard, whilst a couple of locomotives went to Newport Ebbw Junction for trials on iron-ore trains between Newport Docks and the Spencer Steelworks. Two further Type 3s were to be found working in multiple on fitted mineral trains from the Eastern Valleys to the steelworks at Llanwern and Margam, with two more at Landore for similar trials from Margam to Trostre Steelworks.

Landore diesel depot was officially opened on 6 May 1963 and D6820-3/31/3 were amongst its first residents. By July 1963, the EE Type 3s were permitted over most routes in South Wales, and 18 freight diagrams were allocated from Newport (Ebbw Junction) depot. Another freight duty had taken members of the class from Carmarthen to Aberystwyth, over the line through Strata Florida, that would be closed completely within 18 months.

Further transfers and deliveries to Landore by September 1963 brought the total of the type there to 14, with duties taking them to Pembroke Dock, Milford and Neyland (depot closed 9 September 1963). D6853 went as driver training locomotive to Tondu shed, where nine of the class were employed by the following May.

Back on the Eastern Region, the Stratford-based Type 3 diagram covering the Harwich (Parkeston Quay) to Liverpool Central boat train, was extended to take the diesel beyond Sheffield Victoria to Guide Bridge. Thus, a regular daytime diesel working over the electrified Sheffield to Manchester 'Woodhead' route was established. Other changes in the pattern of diesel working during the summer months of 1963 included the replacement of Brush Type 2 diesels on the King's Cross-Cleethorpes expresses, and a through working each Friday night from Manchester to Yarmouth, the latter a Sheffield (Darnall) duty.

On 19 June 1963, D6847 piloted D40 into Plymouth on the down 'Cornishman', making what is believed to be the Type 3s' first appearance in Devon. The next day, D6847 joined forces with D23 on the 4.00pm Plymouth-Manchester.

Although the class had been accepted, and later repaired, at both Doncaster and Darlington Works, they began to appear at Crewe Works from late 1963, D6769 being in

Above:
Class 37 has also put in a lot of work moving freight in East Anglia. Among such turns have been cross-London freights, such as the 10.45 Willesden to Ripple Lane, seen here at Leytonstone on 28 October 1987 with No 37131 in charge. *Paul Shannon*

Top:
The Sheffield area used its allocation primarily for freight. This activity often involved traversing the Woodhead route to make forays into the yards on the periphery of East Manchester. No D6815, still in green, but with all-yellow nose ends, passes Bullhouse with a westbound engineers' train in November 1969. *L. A. Nixon*

Centre:
Some examples were based at Wath for a short time. They were not, however, equipped with the slow speed control gear needed for working merry-go-round (MGR) trains through discharge points. Notwithstanding this, No 37020 is seen at the head of a rake of HAA hoppers at Manvers Main Colliery, joining the Doncaster to Barnsley line from the Swinton and Knottingley Joint route. *L. A. Nixon*

Above:
The Doncaster area has seen a great deal of Class 37 activity down the years. On 7 June 1972 No 6814 approaches the station. *D. I. Rapson*

Above:
No 37019 takes the crossover in Doncaster station on 7 May 1976 with an up oil train, probably heading for Immingham. *D. I. Rapson*

the yard there on 10 November. Thereafter, some interesting cavalcades could be viewed crossing the Pennines, not the least being Class 9F 2-10-0 92010 dragging D250, D237 and D6766 through Huddersfield on 30 December 1963 and former Midland Railway 4F 0-6-0 43906 in charge of D6756 (nearly 50 years its junior) on 2 January 1964. In mid-February, no fewer than seven Type 3s were under repair at Crewe. Whilst the class has never been associated with Swindon Works, D6910 was reported as being inside the stock shed there in December 1963.

The final 12 of the class to be constructed at RSH Darlington were delivered during the first five months of 1964. D6898 (noted at Doncaster Works on 6 May) was the very last locomotive to be built at the Robert Stephenson & Hawthorn Works. By this time, the rate of delivery from Vulcan Foundry to Doncaster had been considerably reduced, only D6935/6/7 being received during the months of April and May. This must be considered, however, in the light of the Vulcan workload at the time for, not only had the plant completed and delivered nearly 50 Type 3s during the previous eight months, it had also commenced an engine refurbishing programme on the 'Baby Deltics' (D5900-D5909).

Once D6938 was delivered and accepted, it was sent to Bromsgrove to commence crew training prior to the replacement of the steam banking locomotives there. First recorded there on 3 July 1964, D6938 was to be joined by four sisters before September, thus rendering Bromsgrove shed redundant. A visit on 27 July found D6938, ostensibly allocated to Bath Road, Bristol, taking the place of the Class 9F 'Lickey banker', which was out of use in the shed. Eventually, the diesel takeover was completed and Bromsgrove shed closed in September 1964. By the following spring, Cardiff Canton depot was supplying four Type 3s for banking duties, each being maintained at nearby Worcester shed.

Below:
Having the blue star coupling code meant the class could multiple with a number of other BR classes. On 27 September 1979 No 37094 heads past Benningbrough towards York, in the company of No 25111, with an Up freight. *D. M. Dawber*

Above:
With Class 40 front end, in place of the original, No 37006 propels into Wardley Interchange Sidings with a train from Wearmouth on 20 June 1983. More recently, collision-damaged Nos 37670/1 both received nose ends from scrap Class 40s.
P. J. Robinson

Below:
The type has taken a hand in a variety of one-off movements. During rolling resistance trials along the East Coast main line, two class members were used to propel the prototype Advanced Passenger Train at speeds up to 105mph. This photograph shows No 37101 taking an APT set from Shields depot to Thornaby for attention on 17 October 1983; the location is County Durham. *P. J. Robinson*

Above:
South Wales has always been a stronghold for Class 37, particularly on freight work. No 37241 was the last of the class to retain green livery, although by 10 April 1976, when this photograph was taken, it had lost its lion and wheel emblem. Radyr Yard is the location. *D. I. Rapson*

In December 1966, D6943 was moved from its banking duties at Bromsgrove to replace Worcester's Standard Class 4 4-6-0s on similar work at Honeybourne, rendering assistance to trains climbing Chipping Campden bank. The last EE Type 3 engaged at Bromsgrove was displaced by Hymek D7021, which arrived there on 17 October 1967 to join D7022-4, allowing D6608 to move back to Landore. The story did not end there, however, as the Hymeks found themselves replaced (and subsequently withdrawn) in the spring of 1973, ironically, by EE type 3s (by then Class 37). The Lickey banker was withdrawn at weekends from 7 March 1981 and completely in September 1986.

An inspection saloon traversed the entire length of the Central Wales line (Llanelli to Craven Arms) and on to Shrewsbury on 3 July 1964; Landore-based D6862 providing the motive power. As the train returned south during the late evening, a large headlight was fitted to the locomotive in view of the number of unmanned level crossings on the route.

Within 15 months of the Western Region receiving its first EE Type 3, its allocation had swelled to 120, based largely at Cardiff and Landore but outstationed at virtually all the South Wales sheds and yards from Pembrokeshire to the northern extremities of the Rhondda Valley. At weekends up to 20 locomotives could be found stabled at Newport.

Below:
No 37241 again, this time in blue, arrives at Parc Junction with No 37296 on 2 June 1982 with a train from Ebbw Vale steelworks. *C. R. Holland*

Sixteen trains of ore (loaded to 1,700 tons) were running to Llanwern steelworks each day from Newport Docks, the entire working being diagrammed for four Type 3s. The trains were worked with one locomotive at the front and another at the rear of each train, to facilitate a quick turn-round.

The early autumn of 1964 witnessed the arrival of the first locomotives of a new order for 70 Type 3s from Vulcan Foundry, commencing at D6939. This period also saw an additional car train introduced from the Ford plant at Dagenham to Halewood (near Liverpool), Type 3-hauled between Dagenham and Nuneaton. The inaugural run took place on 18 September in the care of D6707. As 1964 drew to its close, 251 EE Type 3s had entered service over a period of four years and 1965 was to see completion of the order; the total strength of the class was 309 locomotives.

The fish traffic from Hull, which had utilised Type 3 diesels over the Great Central to Leicester, ceased to run in February 1965, although the route still hosted the type on delivery runs from Doncaster to the Western Region. D6976, for instance, was recorded at Nottingham on 21 April 1965, running light engine to its new home at Cardiff. Shortly afterwards, D6977 was exhibited at Marylebone (30 April) to mark the 7th International Congress on Combusion Engines.

The Western Region undertook high-speed tests with paired EE Type 3 locomotives during May and June 1965, the duo working both on the 08.45 'Bristolian', returning to London from Bristol Temple Meads at 12.15. Two pairs of locomotives were used, D6881/D6882 and D6891/D6892, hauling formations of XP64 prototype coaching stock. On 3 June, D6881/2 took an eight-coach train from Paddington to Plymouth and back. In the down direction, the train covered the 173.5 miles to Exeter (via Westbury) in 132min at an average speed of 78.6mph.

The same pairing (D6881/2) made another high-speed run up to Paddington, this time from Swindon, on 27 November 1965, taking over from 7029 Clun Castle on the Western Region's 'Farewell to Steam' special. To conclude the theme of fast running on the Western, another notable incident occurred on 16 May 1967 when a seven-coach rake was substituted for the failed 'South Wales Pullman'. By sheer coincidence, the locomotive provided was D6881, which had worked the trial high-speed runs and now proved its worth conclusively by covering the 113 miles from Patchway to Paddington at an average speed of 79mph.

With the rundown of services via the Great Central, the Type 3s were re-routed, on delivery, via Chesterfield and Derby to Tyseley, and thence to South Wales, D6989/90 being noted at Tyseley on 29 June 1965. Within a few weeks, D6989 had made one of the type's rare appearances on the Southern Region, working a special from Cardiff to Gatwick Airport, via Kensington Olympia (13 August) just a week after D6871 had performed similarly. By the autumn of 1965, the Type 3s found themselves ousted from the York-Bournemouth trains (over the GC) by Tinsley or Immingham Brush Type 4s.

The class was at its full strength of 309 serviceable locomotives for less than a month. Just as the final machine (D6608) was delivered, so D6983 (only seven months old) was destroyed in an accident at Bridgend in the early hours of 19 December 1965. An empty stock train running from Carmarthen to Bristol behind locomotive D1671 ran into the debris caused by a landslip, and almost immediately D6983, hauling a train of empty wagons from Newton Abbot to Margam, collided with D1671. Both locomotives were severely damaged, and subsequently withdrawn.

Once delivery of the Type 3s was complete, they settled down to work successfully in many parts of the British Rail network, notably in South Wales, Yorkshire, the Northeast and the Eastern Counties. A quarter of a century later, those same areas still see regular Class 37 operation, albeit hauling modern freight rolling stock and sporting a variety of liveries. At first, they found themselves working alongside the steam locomotive and sharing their homes at steam sheds from Aberbeeg to North Blyth. The growing allocation of Type 3s to Healey Mills in 1966/67 accelerated the demise of steam traction in the area. The Type 3s had also ousted steam from the Welsh Valleys and East Anglia, and their increased use in Cambridgeshire had hastened the departure of the Britannia Pacifics (to the London Midland Region) in 1963. By 9 September 1967, they had conquered steam traction in the Northeast, where a new diesel depot was under construction at Cambois to allow closure of North and South Blyth steam sheds.

The following year, 1968, witnessed the end of steam on British Rail and the engagement of a handful of EE Type 3s on further test workings. The push-pull trials featuring D6700 are mentioned in Chapter 8, whilst on 13 and 14 March, D6967/68 were to be found hauling air-braked empty stock between Derby and Kettering. During the succeeding two weeks, the same two locomotives (on loan from Stratford depot to the BR Technical Centre at Derby) were used on Westinghouse air brake equipment tests, hauling 99 ferry vans on the Derby-Peak Forest route. They were the longest trains ever run on British Railways.

Type 3 workings over the West Highland line, so commonplace in the 1980s, were a novelty in 1968 when Eastfield's newly-acquired allocation (D6904/5/19/36/7) was used between Glasgow and Fort William on both passenger and freight trains, prior to the Civil Engineer's decision to curtail their use. Thirteen years later they were to return to monopolise West Highland motive power until the coming of the Sprinters in 1989.

Top:
Hereford used to stable several locomotives, particularly at weekends. On 24 March 1973 it was host to two Class 37s (Nos 6925 in green and 6943) and two Class 47s (Nos 1685 and 1588). *David N. Clough*

Above:
Much of the work allotted to the 37s in South Wales has been on coal traffic. In consequence the number of locomotives based in the area, and their movements, have shifted in consort with the changing fortunes of the coal industry. On 15 April 1982 No 37234 passed Tondu with a Nantgarw to Ogmore service. *Paul Shannon*

Top:
Flax Bourton, on the Taunton to Bristol line, is the location where No 37185 was captured by the camera on 13 May 1982 with a special goods heading for Gloucester.
C. R. Holland

Above:
With the decline of Class 25, Cornish freight motive power was placed in the hands of Class 37 from the start of the 1980s. On 2 August 1982 No 37142 arrived at Lostwithiel en route from St Blazey to Fowey Docks. *Paul Shannon*

One of the lesser-chronicled freight turns began in August 1969 when 6712 and 6832 (the use of the 'D' prefix on BR diesels had ceased in the autumn of 1968 upon the cessation of steam working) were used to haul a molten metal train from Cargo Fleet (Teesside) to Consett. The train was made up of Dynamometer Car 4 (DW 150192) and three torpedo wagons with barriers. The British Steel Corporation's intention was to increase the steelmaking capacity at Consett by moving hot metal in these specially designed vehicles which could each convey 130 tons of the substance, although route restrictions limited the capacity to 100 tons. For a while, two trains ran each way per day, but the service did not last long and, a little over a decade later, steelmaking at Consett was but a memory, the final ore train from Redcar running on 10 September 1980 behind 37053 and 37055.

The 1970s was very much a period of consolidation for the Type 3s, which had become known as Class 37 upon the introduction of numerical classification in 1968. The demise of the Western Region's diesel-hydraulic locomotives allowed an opportunity for passenger work which, in turn, necessitated the provision of a train heating boiler. Looking just as comfortable on heavy mineral trains as they did on local trip work and summer Saturday holiday trains, the 37s established a reputation for reliability and honest endeavour.

Their use spread to areas of the London Midland Region, although it is only in recent times they have become common there. Visits to Merseyside, for instance, were incidents of note prior to the 1980s, and appearances on the North Wales coast line were almost unknown, — hence it was surprising to find 37283 (IM) hauling 1E86, the 09.00 Llandudno-York train, on Saturday 3 June 1978. Three weeks later on 25 June, 37223 (CF) headed a charter train to Pwllheli; the first recorded use of an EE Type 3 on the Dovey Junction-Pwllheli stretch of line on the Cambrian system, a portent of things to come. Type 3s did, it should be noted, work to Aberystwyth in the summer of 1966.

Freight workings over the Shrewsbury to Wrexham line were almost commonplace towards the latter part of the 1970s, particularly on trains of slack from South Wales to the British Steel Corporation plant on Deeside. With the cessation of steelmaking at the Deeside Works following the steel strike of 1979-80, there was a need to move stockpiled ore to Llanwern in South Wales. This brought about a daily working for pairs of 37s, commencing on 30 June 1980 when 37187 and 37293 left Shotwick Sidings (Clwyd) with 13 rotary tipplers (100 tonnes capacity). Although loads were soon increased and pairs of Class 56 diesels rostered to operate the service, the 37s returned in 1981 to remove the last of the stockpiled ore. The class has maintained an association with this South to North Wales railway link and 37s are now daily visitors on hot rolled coil trains from Cardiff to Dee Marsh.

The use of Class 37s on iron-ore trains between Port Talbot and Llanwern increased dramatically from 15 March 1976, when the service began to utilise three locomotives hauling 27 100-tonne wagons over part of the South Wales main line. Specially strengthened couplings were fitted to engines dedicated to this service, and so successful were the trials that BR and BSC soon arranged a 12-year contract. As with the movement of ore from North Wales, the 37s were later displaced by pairs of the then-new Class 56 locomotives, though triple-headed Type 3s substituted occasionally thereafter. Triple-heading was mooted for a particularly heavy oil train emanating at Waterston (near Milford Haven) in 1973, and on 16 September that year, the service was noted in West Wales behind Nos 6886, 6996 and 6998.

A couple of years later saw a particularly dramatic event in the history of the class: No 37143 disappeared down an embankment near Marine Colliery, Ebbw Vale on 29 January 1975. A shunting accident caused the locomotive to become derailed and topple over. Despite an abortive attempt to rerail the machine six weeks later, it was not until 4 August 1975 that it was successfully recovered. Eleven years afterwards, 37143 became 37800 Glo Cymru.

A little over a month after this incident, sister locomotives 37218 and 37284 collided at Britannia Colliery. Both suffered severe cab damage, the former not re-entering traffic until the end of June 1978.

A review of depot allocations in January 1978 found Class 37 locomotives at 10 separate sheds, as follows:

Eastern Region (188) — Gateshead (29), Healey Mills (8), Immingham (17), March (39), Stratford (22), Thornaby (45) and Tinsley (28);

Western Region (103) — Cardiff Canton (53) and Landore (50);
Scottish Region (17) — Eastfield (17).

Another depot (Plymouth Laira) was added to the list in February 1978 when 37142 and 37267 were transferred in, from Landore and Stratford respectively. Driver training commenced that month as a prelude to their use on china clay diagrams in Cornwall, and both were to be found at St Blazey during March.

In February 1980, Landore depot completed its first overhaul and repair of a Class 37 diesel, 37258 being the machine in question. At this time, two dozen of the class were away at either Doncaster or Crewe Works, including five of Landore's own allocation.

At the commencement of the 1981 summer timetable, Class 37 diesels took over most West Highland line duties, sufficient boiler-fitted examples having been transferred to Scotland during the previous winter. Eastfield depot had 25 of the class on its books at the turn of the year, and the May diagrams involved the use of 11 locomotives each day for both freight and passenger work. Unfortunately, during inclement conditions in the following winters, the class was beset by wheelslip problems.

On 28 May 1981, Landore-based 37180 became the first of the class to be named when a former Chairman of Dyfed Council, Mr Tom George, bestowed the name *Sir Dyfed County of Dyfed* at Carmarthen station. Later in the year, four of the West Highland locomotives were named at Glasgow Queen Street, and subsequent naming data can be found elsewhere in this publication. Some 18 years earlier, nameplates had been fitted to D6703/4/7, though none was ever unveiled and all were removed within a few months.

Use of 37s in pairs was quite common on a variety of trains ranging from heavy freight to railtours. Double-headed units could be found as far afield as East Anglia (Freightliners), the West Midlands (100-ton oil trains), on stone trains to Wolverton and on merry-go-round (MGR) coal workings in South Wales, to give but a few examples, the latter particularly noticeable following the introduction of such traffic into Aberthaw late in 1979. The Hunterston to Ravenscraig iron-ore trains have long been in the care of such motive power as, more recently, has been the Lackenby to Corby 'Tubeliner'. Similarly, the Cumbrian Coast line was visited by pairs of Type 3s earlier this decade on trains of steel blooms from Lackenby to Workington, whilst Shap summit still sees its daily train of 'Clyde Cement' hoppers and tanks running between Clitheroe and Gunnie (Coatbridge), 37-powered since 1982, and Preston Docks receives a double-headed oil train from Lindsey.

A year after their West Highland takeover, the 37s infiltrated the Far North and could be found at Wick and Thurso from May 1982. 37183 (the first 37 to reach Thurso — 3 May 1982) was at Kyle of Lochalsh for driver familiarisation a week later, although Class 26 diesels continued to operate the services to Inverness. Initially, 37s did not work Inverness-Aberdeen trains but 37265 (ED) was at Aberdeen for crew training in October 1982. Nine of the class were allocated to Inverness at the end of the year, all fitted with the requisite headlamps and radio aerials.

The visit to this country by Pope John Paul II over the 1982 Spring Bank Holiday generated much extra revenue for BR and some Class 37 locomotives found themselves busily engaged on passenger work hauling special trains conveying passengers going to see the Pope. Notable in this respect were 37090 in South Wales and 37073 in Scotland.

For the third successive summer, Class 37 diesels were involved in major changes on West Highland passenger routes. This time it was the coming of the 'Ethels', three former Class 25 locomotives converted to mobile generators, which in 1983 were coupled behind a Class 37 train engine to provide heat upon the introduction of the Mk III sleeping cars on the West Highland line. 37191 headed the first train of Mk III sleepers out of Glasgow Queen Street on 3 October 1983 with 97251 *Ethel 2* in tow, although previously use had been made of *Ethel* units on Edinburgh-Oban excursions on several Sundays in July and September 1983.

More than 20 years after their introduction on the Liverpool Street to King's Lynn services, the summer timetable of 1983 brought to an end the rostering of Class 37s on this route. Suitably decorated with a smart headboard, 37052 worked the 14.36 from Liverpool Street and 17.30 return on 14 May 1983. The previous afternoon, appropriately Friday 13th, had witnessed the final day of freight services over the Settle and Carlisle line. Despite the 37s never having been closely associated with this route, it is worthy of

Top:
No 37207 was the first of Laira's allocation to be named, receiving *William Cookworthy* nameplates shortly before this picture was taken on 29 July 1982. The train is at Drinnick Mill, on its way to Parkendillock.   *Paul Shannon*

Above:
The Scottish Region did not receive any examples from new but acquired a small fleet in the mid-1960s for freight traffic, mainly in the Central Lowlands. In this illustration No 37142 heads south along the East Coast main line with empty carflats forming a Bathgate to Ripple Lane working on 21 July 1986.   *N. E. Stead*

note that 37048 — en route to Doncaster Works — was coupled behind 40196 on the very last freight to traverse the 'Long Drag'.

Early in 1984 it was expected that Crewe Works would perform all major overhauls on the class, with the possible exception of collision repairs. A survey of BR workshops in mid-January found 37050/5 under repair at Stratford, 37071, 37133/94 and 37220 at Doncaster Works and 37005/38/84/8, 37107/75/98, 37221/9/54/64/94 at Crewe. By the spring, only 28 of the class remained to be dual braked, whilst after suffering collision damage (caused by a tree!) 37183 was sent to Swindon Works for repair, as was 37146.

The 'Highland Rail' emblem adorned 37260 when it was named at Dingwall on 7 July 1984 as part of the radio signalling launch on the Dingwall to Kyle of Lochalsh line, extension of which has since seen radio electronic token block infiltrate the Far North line and the consequent removal of semaphore signals. During the next few weeks, Thornaby-based 37059 illustrated the versatility of the class, deputising for a 47/7 on the

Top:
The class has taken a hand in freight movements along the Stranraer route. Maybole is the place where No 37250 was photographed on the 11.43 Stranraer to Tyne Yard on 17 July 1984. *Paul Shannon*

Above:
Parcels traffic for Stranraer adds to the variety of work allocated to the class. Closeburn, on the Carlisle to Kilmarnock railway, was where No 37036 was caught at the head of the service from London on 23 August 1985. *D. M. Dawber*

11.00 Glasgow-Edinburgh (push-pull) on 12 July, only to be found in Carmarthen on the 31st!

 Undoubtedly 1985 was a year of major happenings, highlighted by the entry into traffic of 37401/3/4, which emerged from Crewe Works on 28 June, freshly overhauled and fitted with electric train heating equipment for use in Scotland. The class began to appear regularly on the Chester-Holyhead main line on trials, initially with the Crewe test stock and later piloting the booked locomotive (a Class 33) on the 11.15 Crewe-Bangor. The first glimpse of such an unlikely combination was on 9 October 1985 when 37411 ran in tandem with 33005 to Chester. A new regime began on the Cambrian Coast, with a pair of 37s designated to haul the 07.30 from Euston between Shrewsbury and Aberystwyth (37124+37186 worked the first such train on 18 May) and two single 37s diagrammed to the 07.53 Shrewsbury-Aberystwyth and the 09.35 ex-Euston. 37196 became the first of its type to receive the grey and yellow Railfreight livery, while for the purpose of filming a TV advertisement 37093 was temporarily repainted to resemble a

Top:
It was not until the 1980s that Class 37 displaced Class 27 on both passenger and freight diagrams on the West Highland. The advent of ETS coaching stock, in place of steam heating, brought the provision of ETHELs to supply the necessary power until ETS-equipped Class 37/4s took over. In this shot, taken at Bridge of Orchy, No 37012, fitted with mini snowploughs, has an ETHEL in tow. *P. J. Robinson*

Above:
Class 37/4 arrived in 1985 and offered benefits to both passenger and freight timetables. Firstly, the need for ETHELS was removed, whilst the higher tractive effort removed the need for double-heading on some freight trains. No 37423, of the Railfreight Metals Sector, nears County March, Tyndrum on 25 March 1988 with the 16.34 Glasgow to Fort William. *D. I. Rapson*

Inverness depot painted most of its small fleet in a variation to the Eastfield livery.
No 37260 show the style, including Highland stag emblem on the cab side. Diesel fuel
pours out of the tank as it leaves Perth with a DMU in tow, bound for Dundee on
15 September 1986. *D. I. Rapson*

Inverness used its fleet to replace Class 26 on Far North and Far West trains. No 37264
stands at Kyle of Lochalsh with the 11.28 service. *David N. Clough*

Top:
By 1985 Class 37/4 had replaced Class 37/0 north of Inverness. No 37414 approaches Achanalt on 30 August 1988 with the 07.10 Kyle to Inverness, as rain pours on to the nearby hillside. *David N. Clough*

Above:
Thurso station in August 1988 finds No 37415 waiting to set off for Georgemas Junction with the 18.14 to Inverness on 30 August 1988. *David N. Clough*

Tinsley-based examples began to appear on the Buxton stone traffic in the early 1980s. Initially this was on the daily working to Salford. On 2 July 1984, Nos 37113+106 pass Buxworth whilst returning from Salford Hope Street to Tunstead. *D. M. Dawber*

police car! May 1985 also saw the launch of the 'Royal Scotsman' — a land cruise definitely designed for the wealthy and entrusted to Class 37 haulage, whilst 37007+37178 spared the blushes of the GW150 committee after both steam locomotives had failed on the 'Great Western Limited' celebration train on 7 April.

At the end of the year, the first 21 locomotives in the 37/4 sub-class had been outshopped, and 1986 saw the emergence of sub-Class 37/5, 37501-7 being put to traffic by the end of April. These were the first of the refurbished freight examples (Brush equipment, Series I design) and they entered traffic with 37698/9 (Brush equipment, Series 2 design). Later in the year the remaining variants of 37/7 and 37/9 began to emerge from Crewe Works and by January 1987, 36 life-extended units had entered traffic, including four of the planned six Class 37/9s of 1,800hp. Not until March 1989 was the refurbishment programme completed, 37719 (formerly 37033) being the 135th candidate for this work at Crewe.

The Kyle line received its first 37/4s on 8 January 1986, when 37417 (on the 10.55 from Inverness) and 37418 (17.55 ex-Inverness) made their debut, just two weeks after 37419 had put in an appearance at — of all places — Wisbech! This followed tests of the sub-class at Derby RTC. Not until 29 January did the Far North line welcome a 37/4, when 37421 was employed on the 06.35 Inverness-Thurso.

The next event featured a naming ceremony at Motherwell to celebrate the introduction of the first two dedicated locomotives for Scottish steel traffic, when titles were bestowed upon newly-renumbered 37310/1. During August 1985, some of the

Motherwell allocation found themselves double-heading MGR trains from Hunterston to Spring's Branch (Wigan) with coal destined for Fidler's Ferry power station near Warrington. The first run of this short-lived traffic was made on 19 August 1985 behind 37034+37151.

From 12 May 1986, the famous 'Cambrian Coast Express' title was revived and the inaugural 07.22 Aberystwyth-Euston, with newly-named 37426 at its head, heralded the return of a daily loco-hauled working on the Cambrian line. The last six 37/4s (37426-37431), having been allocated to Cardiff Canton, began regular operation over this route, assisted on summer Saturday trains by 37/0s and the occasional Railfreight 37/5.

Although 37693, released from Crewe on 27 July 1986, was part of the Cardiff fleet, it was recorded in East Anglia on 2 September and at Oban a week later, thus emulating stablemate 37509 which had teamed up with 25109 on a Westbury to Uddingston special on 22 August, and been entrusted with the 06.05 Carlisle to Glasgow Central the following day. In a similar vein, 37426 was way off its Cambrian diagram when hauling Glasgow & South Western passenger services in early September. By way of a footnote, 37693 was transferred to Thornaby on 14 September, becoming the first refurbished 37 on the Eastern Region.

Within days of their release to traffic, 37796 and 37803 were used on trial workings with a view to replacing the short-lived 20/3 sub-class on Tunstead to Northwich stone trains. For a time they were loaned to Buxton depot, before moving on to Cardiff, and within a few months, Tinsley-based 37/5s (37676-37688) had become staple power at the Derbyshire depot. During the winter, the Welsh 37/4s migrated to coal duties and were joined by the first of the 1,800hp 37/9s. Eleven of the series one 37/5 sub-Class (37501-37511) were transferred from Cardiff to Thornaby, the latter losing some 37/0 examples to Tinsley and Eastfield. Authorisation was forthcoming for more 37/7 conversions with the North Thames-side petroleum traffic in mind.

Whilst running round its train of Strathclyde electric multiple-unit stock at Westerton on 30 January 1987, 37011 was en route to Dalmuir Park to cross over, when the EMUs ran away and caught up with the 37 at Singer. The resultant damage brought about 37011's demise; this was only the second withdrawal of a Class 37 in their 26-year history. This tally was doubled in March 1989 with the condemnation of 37062 and 37113, though the latter was to be reinstated later at the expense of 37260.

Despite the class being spread liberally between Thurso and Penzance, the use of 37s on the Southern Region has been very limited, other than to Micheldever on oil trains and the occasional excursion. Therefore, the sudden appearance of 37s on the Chessington branch (37222 was the first on 19 January 1987) came as something of a

Above left:
Three locomotives for four wagons, a very high power-to-weight ratio! The train is the Briggs Sidings to Ashburys trip, with Nos 37296, 45060 and 25078, the first two bound only for Peak Forest for other stone duties. *Steve Turner*

Above:
Class 37 appearances on passenger trains in the Northwest have included the summer Saturday extras to Blackpool which started on the Eastern Region. On 18 June 1983 No 37174 sets off from Bolton with the 13.59 Blackpool North to Castleford.
Paul Shannon

Below:
On 4 May 1985, when West Coast main line trains were being diverted via the Settle and Carlisle route, sufficient Type 4 motive power was difficult to find. This brought No 37095 on to the 10.43 Carlisle to Leeds, seen here at Garsdale. Note the radiator outer grille mesh has been removed, a policy on both the ER and ScR. *David N. Clough*

Above:
Appearances on the Southern Region have been quite common. One of the services which was diagrammed for them was the 10.22 Didcot to Orpington coal train, pictured at Tolworth amid snow on 21 January 1987. *Chris Wilson*

surprise. Several more followed, the most notable being 37903 on 9 February. A pair of 37s powered the first freight over the new Felixstowe spur on 16 February 1987.

By August 1987, refurbished engines could be found on five specific traffic flows: on coal trains in South Wales and china clay workings in Cornwall (Laira having received 37669-37675), and on the Buxton stone workings, Northeast steel and North Thames petroleum trains already mentioned. A pair of unrefurbished Buxton-based 'stone' locomotives visited Penmaenmawr Quarry on 20 March 1987 with 21 'Peakstone' hoppers as a curtain-raiser to the use of 37/5s on a weekly train to Manchester (Hope Street). We have already referred to the end of freight traffic over the Settle and Carlisle line, but 37138+37184 were diverted that way on 13 April 1987 with the Clitheroe to Gunnie cement tanks. Cardiff's 37704+37799 ran trials on the Hunterston to Ravenscraig circuit in May, whilst March depot lost its allocation of the class, and with it an assocation stretching back a quarter of a century, in May 1987.

The new Railfreight livery of dark and light grey, with colourful sub-Sector embellishments, was unveiled in October 1987 and 37892 was subsequently displayed in immaculate external condition, and sporting the Petroleum sub-Sector livery, at Ripple Lane Open Day. 37673, which had been kept under wraps at Stratford, was unveiled for official photographs sporting Speedlink Distribution colours.

Commencing in March 1988, 22 unrefurbished Class 37s were fitted with regeared CP7 bogies (37350-37359, 37370-37381), whilst repainting continued in a somewhat haphazard fashion. Without doubt, 1988 was a more settled year than the previous three had proved to be. Changes in Scotland saw 37401 receive InterCity livery and 37423 repainted into Railfreight colours, whilst the ominous influx of Sprinters at Haymarket and Inverness signalled the next round of changes in the fluctuating history of the English Electric Type 3 locomotive, with their impending displacement from many passenger services.

Chapter 2

The Life-Extension Programme

When the switch from steam to diesel power on BR was being planned, it was not originally intended to build any modern traction in the power bracket 1,500 to 2,000hp. However, the need was soon perceived for motive power of this capability and three designs were eventually taken forward. The one favoured by central management was that put forward by the English Electric Co, which was intended as a system-wide standard. The Southern and Western Regions had other preferences and the upshot was the construction of the Birmingham Railway Carriage & Wagon Type 3s (now Class 33) and the Beyer Peacock Type 3s (the Hymeks). In fairness, all three proved to be good locomotives. Class 33 has served not only the Southern, but also other Regions well, for over 30 years and proved a versatile machine. The Class 35 Hymeks were the best of the diesel-hydraulics and it was merely the desire to eliminate that form of traction, not any fault in the design, which caused their early withdrawal. The best of the bunch, though, was the English Electric product, the Class 37.

The outline of the class was typical of the company during that period. It featured rugged construction and a stepped-front profile which was once described as 'looking purposeful', rather than eye-catching. Two three-axle bogies spread the 100 tons plus of bulk to give a route availability of 5. Overall weight varied, depending on whether or not a train-heating boiler was fitted. The diesel fitted was the most advanced form then available of the old stalwart 'V' engine. Designated the 12 CSVT, it had charge air cooling, to offer higher power per cylinder, and EE offered it at 2,025bhp. The railways preferred a more conservative figure and so it was set to develop 1,750bhp. The main generator was bolted to the engine and supplied traction motors of the same type as those being used for the 3,300hp Deltics. Having to cope with only half the power that the same parts did in their larger brethren, it is not surprising that these components have never given trouble.

Indeed, their trouble-free nature has been a hallmark of the Class 37s. Availability soon settled down to between 85 and 90% and reliability was usually between 30,000 and 40,000 miles per casualty; very few other classes came close to, let alone bettered, this standard. 25 years of service, though, takes its toll and the usual cycle of works repair of major components is no longer sufficient to keep performance up to the required standard. The reliability measure had begun to decline for this reason by the start of the 1980s. Constraints on investment by BR meant that a rolling programme of traction and rolling stock renewal had never been adhered to and in consequence a significant proportion of the fleet would be over a quarter of a century old by 1990, with no proven replacements in sight. The problem had already been tackled with Classes 31, 47 and 50, which were receiving general overhauls; life extension to the mid-1990s was the aim.

Since Class 37 had been such a useful workhorse, consideration was given to undertaking a life-extension programme on a larger scale, as examination of the physical condition of the fleet indicated it would be suitable for use into the next century. Sector-led management was coming into play in the early 1980s when the Class 37 life-extension programme was being considered, and a need was perceived for three variants of the type to fulfil specific duties. These were: electric train heating-equipped units for some passenger work; a 'heavyweight' locomotive, which could develop a starting tractive effort equal to a Class 56; and a general purpose RA5 locomotive for the remaining work. The British Railways Board engineers then drew up an engineering specification to meet these demands and the heavy general repair (HGR) or refurbishment programme was born.

From the above it will be seen that whereas before there had been essentially just one type of Class 37, which either had a steam heat capability or not, for the future this uniformity would be lost. As the programme was in progress, capital was not always available to give each locomotive falling due for works repair a HGR and eventually the decision was taken to fit overhauled, but unrefurbished, examples with the modified

Above:
Class 37 was constructed in the workshops of the English Electric Co at Vulcan Foundry and Robert Stephenson & Hawthorn. This 1961 official photograph shows the fitting of a power unit in one of Vulcan's build. *GEC Traction*

bogies (designated CP7) being fitted as part of the HGR scheme. This gave rise to yet another sub-class. With a view to trying out possible diesels for the next generation of Type 3s, some units undergoing HGR were to receive a different engine and the final sub-type emerged.

Before describing the work entailed in the programme it is worth setting out here the various forms in which Class 37 now appears:

Class 37/0 – standard, as-built locomotives;
Class 37/3 – Class 37/0, except fitted with CP7 bogies;
Class 37/4 – Class 37/5, except fitted for electric train heat supply (ETS);
Class 37/5 – HGR overhauled unit, retaining RA5;
Class 37/7 – Class 37/5, except ballasted up to 120 tonnes, giving RA7;
Class 37/9 – Class 37/7, except fitted with experimental diesel engines.

Technical differences between these types can be identified in Appendix 2 at the end of the book.

As-built, some technical differences existed between locomotives. Those fitted with nose-end gangway doors from new, Nos 37001-119, are designated Series 1. In consequence, the arrangement of the equipment in the nose end differs in these locomotives from those in the remainder of the class. Series 2 is applied to the next batch of locomotives, which had centrally positioned headcode boxes. Series 3 covers the last 50 examples. These have the same nose end layout as Series 2 but important differences in part of the control schematic. A voltage balance wheelslip circuit replaced the previous current balance system, which originated with London, Midland & Scottish Railway prototype diesel locomotives Nos 10000-1. Wheelslip detection and correction was a weakness in the first two series of Class 37 and the last series were an improvement. This system is fitted during the HGR programme to all those machines not already so equipped. Series 3 machines also have an uprated wiring schematic. To make it easier for depot staff to identify Series 1 and 2/3 (as they are described) builds apart, a numbering system following a HGR was devised to take account of this. Thus Nos 37501 upwards and 37701-800 are Series 1, whilst Nos 37699 downwards and 37801-99 are Series 2 and 3 types. All machines in the Class 37/4 and 37/9 sub-classes came from the last two series.

The HGR work has, to date, all been carried out at BREL's Crewe Works. When a locomotive arrives it is completely gutted to allow some components to be repaired,

Above:
Until the start of the refurbishment programme, all works repairs were carried out at Doncaster. The works retains responsibility for some of the CEM work carried out on the class. No 37209 is seen in works on 7 August 1988 undergoing an F exam. *Steve Turner*

others to be replaced and the interior shell to be worked on. This is cleaned fully and, in the case of Class 37/7, it is at this time that steel slab ballast weights are fitted. Before component replacement a full internal repaint is carried out. The exterior of the body receives such attention as is needed to remove corrosion. The nose end doors fitted to Series 1 are welded up to remove them as a source of cab draughts. Indicator boxes are removed from Series 1, whilst blanking plates are fitted to the former headcode panel for Series 2; in both cases marker lights are fitted. A high visibility headlight is fitted at each end. Finally, the grilles on each side of the nose end are modified to a uniform large size to ensure sufficient air supply to the traction motor blowers, preventing air being drawn from the cab and causing draughts.

The cab environment comes in for attention, but the same driving position and controls are retained. Better insulation in the engine room bulkhead and round the doors cuts down noise, whilst better thermal insulation is provided around the driver's kneehole position to cut down draughts. Seats of a better standard are fitted, whilst instrumentation, in particular its illumination, is improved. In the past, drivers would sometimes fail a locomotive due to poor lighting of the gauges at night. A speed-sensing device is incorporated to allow one-man operation. Revised windscreen washing and wiping equipment is installed, together with windscreen glass of a toughness up to UIC (International Union of Railways) standards.

Some important changes have been introduced in the engine room. The main generator has not been trouble-free. As a result of changing the brush gear, devoting greater attention to the generator during maintenance (especially to earth fault detection), and following improved procedures in the BREL shops where major repairs are effected, this component has become less of a problem. It was considered worthwhile, though, to replace it with AC power generation equipment; this would be more reliable and cheaper to run. Whilst the majority of the alternators fitted are of Brush manufacture, some of GEC origin have been fitted; the latter are found in locomotives numbered either side of No 37800. A main and auxiliary alternator have their outputs rectified by main and auxiliary rectifiers. For Class 37/4, the auxiliary machines are dual wound to provide the ETS.

The alternator frame is mounted on the engine but is separated from the rectifiers by a bulkhead, fitted to segregate the engine from the electrical and electronic components; this has created a clean air compartment, which saves the electrics from being contaminated by the dirty, oily atmosphere produced by the diesel. Engine starting now has to be provided by two Bosch motors of the type used in Classes 56 and 58. A new electronic equipment frame replaces the original load regulator and resistors. It contains

Above:
General illustration inside Crewe Works on 28 September 1985 shows the programme well under way. Visible are Nos 37292/278/299/267/269/266/271/297/291/296.
David N. Clough

the voltage regulator (AVR), load regulator, field divert control unit, temperature detector and, if fitted, a slow speed control (SSC) unit; wiring for SSC is included in all locomotives as part of the HGR. The new AVR ensures better battery charging. Mention has been made of the relative inadequacy of the wheelslip control system fitted to Series 1 and 2 units. The voltage balance system fitted new to Series 3 examples, and incidentally similar to that used in Class 56, has now been adopted as standard for the whole class.

Two changes affect the cooler group. The radiator fan is driven by a shaft off the free end of the engine. In the original design its speed was dependent on engine speed, not cooling system temperature. This often meant that locomotives which spent a lot of time standing with engine running would be overcooled and liable to fuel dilution. A temperature-controlled clutch is being fitted to the shaft, which can disengage it if there is no need for the fan to be driven. In some instances the system header tank was life-expired, so the opportunity has been taken to fit a new one of larger capacity, which also has the advantage of reducing the risk of engine shutdown due to low coolant.

Wiring of the latest specification has replaced all the original material: it is now carried in trunking, above floor level where possible. Better interior lighting has been incorporated. The air filtration system using oil-wetted units is being replaced by dry pack material of the type used in Class 56 and other modern designs. Filtered air is supplied to the engine and clean air compartments and the traction motor blowers in the nose ends. Where still in place, the steam generating boiler is removed. Under the locomotive, the tank formerly used to store water for the boiler has been converted to an additional fuel tank, giving a useful extension to the working range. If the tanks are in poor condition they are replaced. Brackets to enable miniature snowploughs to be carried are fitted as standard.

Mention has been made that modified bogies designated CP7 are fitted. As the sector managers felt a top speed of 80mph was satisfactory for all planned work, including passenger traffic, this enabled the traction motors to be geared down, giving better starting and low speed characteristics. What this means is that where before the motors could run up to about 130mph without risk of bursting due to rotational forces, this limit has now dropped to around the 100mph mark. In order to cope with the extra weight of a Class 37/7, wheelsets of the Class 50 pattern are fitted to all CP7 bogies, regardless of the locomotive under which they are installed. This maintains interchangeability. Refurbished traction motors are used but, as they have bored-out axleways, they are redesignated as Type 538/5A motors, the same as Class 50. Medium speed sanding gear substitutes for the original type, as adhesion is very important when hauling heavy trains. To obtain the benefits of the CP7 bogie, some examples entering works for an Intermediate overhaul, as opposed to a HGR or an F exam, were also fitted with them and became Class 37/3.

A standard repair is given to the diesel, the cooler group and the remainder of the bogies not affected by conversion to the CP7 type. Twelve members of the class required the fitting of train air brake gear to complete that particular programme. All this work takes about 21 weeks and is concluded by a full repaint. No 37268 was the first to enter Crewe on 22 June 1984 for conversion to No 37401. As the Scottish Region wished to eliminate steam heating before the winter 1985 timetable came into force, the target was to get 24 Class 37/4s in traffic by that date, hence the reason why this sub-class appeared before any of the freight ones. Although seven more of this sub-class emerged, six went from works to Cardiff Canton, rather than Scotland as originally planned, for use on the Cambrian. These were turned out concurrently with the first few Class 37/5s, commencing with No 37698. Freight sector needs dictated whether the remainder emerged as Class 37/5 or Class 37/7. Eight of the WR's fleet, Nos 37796-803, received GEC alternators instead of the Brush equipment fitted to all other machines.

The refurbishment programme has been a success. For example, take the greater productivity achieved by Class 37/7s on trainload coal and steel traffic in South Wales. Their greater adhesion enabled a single locomotive to handle 28 HAA wagons on the Aberthaw jobs where before two Class 37/0s were needed for 35 wagons. In mid-1987 Nos 37799+803 were trialled on the iron ore services between Port Talbot and Llanwern; these were sequels to earlier trials using Class 37/9s.

Unfortunately a loose traction motor pinion (previously unknown with Class 37) curtailed the trial running. Nevertheless, on 9 September 1987 Nos 37895+799 took the full 3,060-tonne load normally diagrammed for two Class 56s. This trial went to serve as proof that Class 37s could reliably displace the Type 5s on these duties, and the switch came about from May 1988, albeit with concurrent introduction to slower schedules. Targets of 78% availability and 30,000 miles per casualty apply. In the previous climate of financial targets Railfreight needs to get a combination of maximum tractive effort per pound spent, coupled with as little down-time as possible and minimum repair costs.

Performance has been up to expectations. The electrical machines have required less maintenance work than the old main generator. Some electrical control problems have occurred, whilst Eastfield has suffered with starter motor failures.

It will be interesting to see how the replacement diesels used in Class 37/9 fare, with close attention being paid to whether or not they prove more reliable than the original Class 37 engine.

Taken overall, refurbishing has been a big benefit. Although it had been envisaged that all the fleet would ultimately undergo a HGR, shortage of money cut back the number of locomotives put through the programme in some years, slowing the programmes down. After the placing of the Class 60 order, there was less need for HGR units and so the cost of putting locomotives through the refurbishment programme became less easy to justify. This brought the programme to an end, the last machine to pass through Crewe Works being No 37719, which emerged on 20 March 1989. A total of 135 members of the class have been refurbished, the sub-class breakdown being:

Class 37/4 31
Class 37/5 54
Class 37/7 44
Class 37/9 6

Below:
Each locomotive was gutted to the basic shell, as can be seen in this shot of No 37066.
David N. Clough

Above:
Side view of nose ends of as-built Class 37s on Bristol Bath Road. To provide better ventilation for the equipment in the nose ends, the grilles on the second man's side were enlarged during the life-extension process. *C. R. Holland*

Below:
After the work had been completed, each machine was given a trial run from Crewe to Llandudno, hauling a rake of test stock. No 37691 is pictured at Sandycroft on its return journey on 6 February 1987. *D. I. Rapson*

Chapter 3

The Class 37/9 Project

In February 1985 GEC Diesels approached BR with a request for facilities for field trials of its six-cylinder RK270T diesel. Towards the middle of that year, Hawker Siddeley Group made a similar approach for its Mirrlees MB275T engine. At this time the BR plans for its future motive power procurement envisaged a new Class 38 diesel electric, which would be rated at between 1,800 and 2,100bhp. Both the above manufacturers were therefore keen to demonstrate products which would feature in any proposal they would submit, when BR finally put the Class 38 out to tender. It will be recalled that No 47046 had been converted to No 47601 and later No 47901 to provide a test-bed for the Ruston 16-cylinder diesel intended for Class 56 and then the Ruston 12-cylinder variant planned for Class 58.

The Director, Railfreight gave his permission for the necessary conversion work on Class 37s within that Sector. Whilst the BRB naturally retained overall control of the project, responsibility for the detailed design work involved rested with each manufacturer. The initial plan was that fitting out of the locomotives selected for Mirrlees engines would be done at the Brush Works at Loughborough (Mirrlees and Brush both being part of the Hawker Siddeley Group), while the Vulcan Works was chosen for the installation work on the Ruston units. If this plan had been carried out, the fitting of the Ruston diesels would have taken the Class 37s involved back to the factory in which they were built. But, as neither works was rail-connected at this time, the simplest option was to carry out the fitting at BREL's Crewe site as part of the

Below:
The combined Ruston diesel and GEC Traction main alternator are seen prior to installation. *British Railways Board*

34

life-extension programme — accordingly, BREL was contracted by both manufacturers
to handle this part of the operation.

Hawker Siddeley offered four Mirrlees units for trial and these were fitted at
Loughborough with the standard Brush alternator being used as part of the
life-extension programme; the power unit assembly then went to Crewe for installation.
The Mirrlees diesel is a six-cylinder in-line engine and has been set to deliver 1,800bhp
at 1,000rpm. Ruston offered two of its diesels and these received GEC Traction
alternators at Vulcan Works, the type being used in a total of 10 life-extended Class 37s.
The RK270T has been set to develop 1,800bhp at 900rpm. Both diesels have a nominal
rating of 2,400bhp.

To minimise the design changes needed, all six prototypes were selected from
Series 2 Class 37s due for overhaul. Some modifications were needed in connection
with the change from the 12CSVT diesel. The MB275T is a longer, taller and heavier
machine than its EE predecessor. This meant that the underframe needed alteration to
accept the alternator feet. Consequent upon this was a need to alter the air
management, as the air ventilating the alternator could no longer be exhausted through
the alternator could no longer be vented through the underframe; instead it now vents
into the engine compartment. Piping and cable trunking have needed rerouteing, whilst
the reduced space between the engine and cooler group bulkhead forced a relocation of
the brake equipment frame to the clean air compartment. Other minor modifications
were also needed.

As the RK270T is lighter than its older stablemate, the flexible mounting needed
modification. The brake equipment frame has also been resited to the clean air
compartment. Being more compact than the 12CSVT, access for maintenance is easier.
The higher turbocharger temperatures at which both diesels operate brought an
enforced change to engine cooling arrangements. Both manufacturers opted for Spiral
tube radiator panels, but the radiator fan in the Ruston-equipped examples has been
regeared at a higher speed. This change was accomplished by using a gearbox from a
scrap Class 40. The need to comply with UIC noise regulations meant a silencer had to
be fitted. This was to be located above the alternator and finding space for a suitable

Top:
One of the first duties diagrammed for the 37/9 sub-class was the movement of steel co[...]
from Llanwern to Shotton. No 37902 passes Dee Marsh Junction on the 02.45 Severn
Tunnel to Dee Marsh Junction on 16 June 1987. *D. I. Rapson*

Above:
Fill-in turns on a variety of services have brought some unusual workings, as recorded
at Newport on 24 October 1988, with No 37904 in charge of a down train of VDBs from
East Usk Yard. This locomotive has been repainted since release from works into the
new Railfreight livery, though without the markings and depot emblems. *M. J. Collins*

design proved difficult. In consequence, both variants have modified roof panels, the Mirrlees ones having a pronounced 'bump'.

Notwithstanding some changes to the control system, both types still retain 'blue star' multiple-unit coupling codes; this means that they can still be jumpered-up with any Class 37, or Classes 20 and 31. Arising from the greater weight of the Mirrlees diesel, it was decided that both types would be ballasted up to a total of 120 tonnes, making them equivalent to Class 37/7 in tractive capability. Since the first batch of Class 37/7s then being turned out of Crewe under the life-extension programme were all going to Cardiff Canton, it was decided to deploy the six prototypes, designated Class 37/9, to that depot as well. Whereas the former were then designated as trainload coal motive power, the latter were intended for steel traffic. To provide for maximum versatility, however, all six were fitted with slow speed control for power station merry-go-round duties.

The contracts with the BRB were for two years, but could be terminated earlier in certain prescribed circumstances. Provision was made for BR to purchase the diesel engines at the end of that term. Both types offer fuel economy over the standard 12CSVT design, as well as lower running costs through reduced servicing. For example, a standard Class 37 receives an A exam after 55hr and a C exam (when the diesel would receive attention) after 825hr; equivalent intervals for the Ruston RK270T are 80 and 1,200hr, whilst for the Mirrlees MB275T they are 100 and 2,000 respectively.

No 37901 had its Mirrlees engine started for the first time on 22 August 1986 and load bank tests on works followed during October. It was released to traffic on 30 October. No 37905, the first of the two Ruston-powered converts was released on 11 December 1986. Subsequently both have been named at Canton, the former *Mirrlees Pioneer*, the latter *Vulcan Enterprise*. Works release dates for all six are as follows:

No 37901   30 October 1986
No 37902   30 October 1986
No 37903   4 February 1987
No 37904   7 April 1987
No 37905   11 December 1986
No 37906   16 December 1986

Trial running was carried out in December 1986 and early 1987. No 37902 took a 1,273-tonne steel coil train from Llanwern to Dee Marsh Junction, returning south with a Crewe to Severn Tunnel Junction freight. No 37905 was used for a similar trial on 20 January 1987 and resulted in the loadings for these services being fixed at 1,300 tonnes. To assess the class's capabilities in comparison with Class 56, on 4 and 5 March 1987, Nos 37905+21 took charge of Port Talbot to Llanwern iron ore services in place of the usual two Class 56s. With the usual 3,060-tonne trailing load the Class 37/9s were able to keep to time as far as Cardiff and managed to restart the train on the 1 in 98 Stormy Bank. This proved a prelude for later trials with Class 37/7s in multiple, which eventually gave rise to them displacing the Class 56 pairings on this traffic.

From 11 May 1987 Class 37/9 was allocated two daily diagrams from Llanwern to Dee Marsh, returning from Crewe to Severn Tunnel Junction, latterly Cardiff Tidal Sidings. They also worked steel traffic to Ebbw Vale. The following year sufficient Class 37/7s were available at Cardiff Canton to allow Type 3s in multiple to replace the previous pairs of Type 5s on the Port Talbot to Llanwern jobs; Class 37/0 was included in the pool of motive power for diagramming purposes.

Service experience has been very good. The silencers proved troublesome initially, bringing a redesign, whilst the Mirrlees variants have proved more prone to control system problems. The intention was always to use these prototypes intensively and this has been the case. During the first two years, the planned project life, the prototypes averaged about 2,100hr per annum on the Total Operations Processing System computer; this compares to 1,700hr for a Class 56 on the WR. In view of the teething problems referred to here, this level of performance is extremely good. In fact, it puts this small sub-class among the most intensively utilised on BR, with probably only Class 47/7 and Class 59 putting in more hours. Should BR ever resurrect the Class 38 project, the experience gained with these six locomotives will prove invaluable and the equipment used in the tests has clearly justified contention for a large order.

Chapter 4

Liveries and Embellishments

The best way to deal with this aspect of the subject is pictorially, the illustrations which follow together with the others in the book, show many of the livery variants carried by Class 37 down the years, whilst Appendix 3 lists the names bestowed.

Above:
Eastfield modified the livery of several of its allocation which were used on West Highland duties. No 37027 was one of them; in this photograph can be seen the nose ends painted yellow and black window surrounds. It also carried a small Scottie dog emblem on the bodyside. On 31 July 1981 the locomotive prepares to leave Glasgow Queen Street at the head of the 16.36 to Mallaig. *David N. Clough*

Right:
Down the years the West Highland fleet has probably witnessed more variation in liveries than any other. Allocated to the InterCity sector, No 37401 received appropriate colours during 1988. In this view, taken on 23 September 1988, it was in charge of a Glasgow to Oban train at Tyndrum Lower. *A. O. Wynn*

Above:
The final version of the Eastfield livery involved the top of the nose ends being painted black, large BR emblem and numbers and a bigger Scottie dog. Note the headlight above the old indicator box, fitted to examples used on the West Highland line. No 37188 was a most unusual visitor to Sheffield. *David N. Clough*

Below:
During July 1983 No 37093 was painted in police colours as part of a BR commercial. The bodyside stripes were in yellow and orange and the whole colour scheme was supposed to wash off — but it didn't, and a full repaint into standard blue was needed. *N. E. Stead*

Top:
Thornaby depot has introduced one or two slight livery variations to its locomotive fleet but none as comprehensive as the repainting of No 37501 in British Steel blue. Its lighter hue is noticeable in contrast to the standard liveried examples in this line-up at the depot in April 1988. *C. R. Holland*

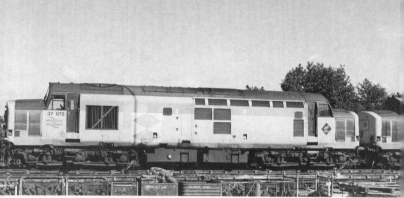

Above:
No 37673 was not returned to traffic straight after being refurbished in April 1987. It was selected for painting in a new three-tone grey sector livery as part of a Railfreight relaunch, planned for October of that year. The three shades of grey are visible here, together with the cast BR and depot emblems; in this case the latter is a Cornish lizard, signifying Laira. Full-width bodyside transfers, denoting the sub-sector allocation also feature; here they are the red and yellow diamonds of Speedlink Distribution. The picture was taken at St Blazey, where No 37673 is based. *David N. Clough*

Top:
Following refurbishment all Class 37/4s were outshopped with a similar livery style to Class 37/5 but in blue, rather than grey and with large bodyside numbers and BR emblems. The ScR transferred names from West Highland Class 37/0s and the bodyside layout can be seen in this illustration of No 37408.   *David N. Clough*

Above:
In some cases, where depots did not have a cast Railfreight emblem, a transfer was applied. This profile of Thornaby's No 37510 shows that depot's kingfisher motif.
David N. Clough

Chapter 5

Class 37 Performance

The changes made to the class as part of the HGR programme have had an impact on the performance specification. It will be useful to summarise here just how the differences translate into road performance.

Table 1: Performance of Class 37 sub-types

Sub-type:	37/0	37/3	37/4
Measurements:			
Max TE (lb)	55,500	56,180	57,440
Continuous TE (lb)	35,000	41,250	41,250
at speed (mph)	13.6	11.4	11.4
Rail hp	1,250	1,254	1,254
Full power range (mph)	10 to 79	7 to 68	7 to 68

The regearing shifts the Class 37/3 performance characteristic to the left, equivalent to the refurbished Class 37s, which have the same gearing. These sub-types offer better performance at low speed which is more appropriate for a freight engine. The as-built specification of Class 37/0 as a mixed traffic prime mover is evident. It is reasonably flexible at low speed, yet offers staying power up to nearly 80mph, which was of assistance for passenger turns covered by the class in their past.

Translating the performance curves into rail horsepower (rhp) will be of benefit for the forthcoming study of the class. The rhp values quoted in Table 1 are those of the continuous rating speed, the one usually used. Power at rail does, however, vary, even within the full power speed range. For Class 37/0, the rhp is fairly consistent at between 1,290 and 1,310 in the 20 to 70mph range. At 80mph it is still 1,270rhp but then tails away as speed rises. The alternator-fitted types (Classes 37/4/5/7) show more fluctuations, producing between 1,295 and 1,320rhp from 20 to 50mph, with a steady fall-off thereafter, giving 1,260 at 60mph, 1,195 at 70mph and 1,115 rhp at 80mph.

Starting off it is fitting to feature a log recorded during their first year of operation and on the line where their first passenger turns were rostered. The data is reproduced from the late C. J. Allen's article in the December 1961 issue of *Trains Illustrated* magazine and was recorded by him from the footplate. The class was taking over this work from the first batch of English Electric Co Type 4s, Class 40, and Mr Allen was not very impressed with the abilities of the smaller Type 3s, even allowing for their lower installed power. Table 2 sets out the log.

Above:
No heating should have been required on 21 June 1975, when No 37035 was caught by the camera passing Stratford on the 11.30 to Norwich.   *Kevin Lane*

Table 2: ER Liverpool Street-Norwich
Locomotive: Type 3 Co-Co diesel No D6715
Load: nine bogies, 304 tons tare, 325 tons gross

Dist		Sched	Actual	Speeds
miles		min	m s	mph
0.00	LIVERPOOL STREET	0	0.00	—
1.25	*Bethnal Green E Jct*	—	3.07	32
			sigs	18*/50
4.00	STRATFORD	8	7.48	44*
7.15	Ilford	—	11.30	62½
10.00	Chadwell Heath	15	14.04	68
12.35	Romford	—	16.23	61
			sigs	30*/2*
14.95	Harold Wood	—	21.18	50
			sigs	32*/20*
18.20	Brentwood	—	25.29	—
19.25	*Milepost 19¼*	—	28.34	36
20.20	SHENFIELD	26	29.48	62½/72
23.65	Ingatestone	—	32.48	69
29.80	CHELMSFORD	35	38.18	60*
32.20	*New Hall*	(3†)	40.38	64½/75
35.95	Hatfield Peverel	—	43.48	72
38.65	WITHAM	46	46.00	73/71½
42.35	Kelvedon	—	49.03	72½/70½
46.70	Marks Tey	53	52.38	80½
		(2†)	pws	20*
51.70	COLCHESTER	60	57.30	—
			pws	25*
54.05	*Parsons Heath*	(3†)	62.22	—
56.05	Ardleigh	—	64.44	60
59.50	MANNINGTREE	71	67.57	71½
63.25	Bentley	74½	71.32	66/67
65.00	*Milepost 65*	—	73.10	61/74
68.80	IPSWICH	81	77.32	—
2.45	*Bramford*	—	3.58	—
4.85	Claydon	—	6.19	64½
8.40	Needham	—	9.29	69
			pws	20*
11.95	STOWMARKET	—	14.25	60
14.25	Haughley	14½	16.51	53
16.20	*Milepost 85*	—	19.10	56½
17.90	Finningham	—	20.43	—
22.70	Mellis	—	23.37	77½
26.30	Diss	—	27.25	82
28.80	Burston	—	29.18	70½
31.90	Tivetshall	29	31.52	72/83½
35.45	Forncett	—	34.38	80½
38.00	Flordon	—	36.30	88/82
41.05	*Swainsthorpe*	—	38.43	85
44.20	*Trowse Upper Jct*	(2†)	41.28	35*
45.35	*Trowse*	—	43.16	30*/18*
46.25	NORWICH	46	46.25	—
68.80	Net time (min)	73	69	—
46.25	Net time (min)	46	44	—

* Speed restriction
† Recovery time (min)

Top:
Cross-country Class 37, a not-uncommon sight on summer Saturdays. Deputising for a Type 4, No 37177 passes Radley in charge of the 09.10 Birmingham to Poole on 8 May 1987. *C. R. Holland*

Above:
Holiday traffic has seen many appearances in York station, often replacing a Type 4 for the onward run to Scarborough. On 23 June 1984, No 37186 prepares to leave with a service from Chesterfield. *N. E. Stead*

As far as Shenfield a 60mph limit then applied but signal checks would, in any event, have precluded any fast running. A broken rail at Brentwood meant the following 1 in 85-155 could not be rushed but a recovery to 36mph at the top was good. Four minutes behind time at Shenfield meant a strong incentive to run hard, but the 70mph limit onward to Hatfield Peverel was observed. Full power on the 1 in 222 to Hill House resulted in a drop of only 2mph to 70½mph, and its continued use provided an 80mph maximum in the dip after Marks Tey. After negotiating the Colchester rebuilding scheme, the 2¾ miles of 1 in 145/157 up to Parsons Heath found speed dropping away to 61mph before a concluding burst up to 74mph into Ipswich.

With a temporary speed restriction to contend with, D6715 was only able to recover to 60mph past Stowmarket, and fell back to 53mph on the two miles at 1 in 131 of Haughley Bank. Power was shut off at 80mph on the drop to Mellis and fast running continued, with a peak of 88mph for the trip before eventually slowing for the run into Norwich. On the first stage of the journey, D6715 gained 4min net on a schedule, excluding recovery time, of 73min. On the second stage, the schedule was just maintained.

Moving on to 1965, the WR trials, using two D6700 locomotives provided a portent of things to come in terms of schedules. Permission was given for 100mph running, presumably using selected locomotives having thick tyres, whilst some speed restrictions were relaxed as regards the test train. Mr C. J. Churcher accompanied the run made on 3 June 1965 and he has supplied copies of his diary. D6881+2 were used on a 10-coach rake, comprising five vehicles of the XP64 design.

Reading was passed in 27½min, against 29min booked, and the pair continued to gain time all the way to Exeter, where the arrival was 4½min to the good in a gross time of 132min for the 173.5 miles, equal to a 79mph average. The timing is perhaps best judged alongside the schedule for the 'Cornish Riviera Express' in 1978, when it was at about its quickest when hauled by a single Type 4, which allowed 149min. Continuing to Plymouth, a time of 62min showed a further 2min gain on the booking, with the run from Paddington being completed in a new record of under 196min.

Another record was set on the return, with the 118.4-mile Bristol to Paddington leg being run in 87min, an average of 81.7mph. The maximum for the round trip, 104mph, was made during this section, although 100mph had been reached several times in both directions. It is unfortunate that these trials did not bear fruit straight away in terms of train scheduling. It was not until several years later that the Region used pairs of Class 42 'Warships' to accelerate its principal West of England trains, whilst the advent of the InterCity 125 marked the final development of a high-speed diesel train, using two power cars, but with one at each end of the train. To be fair to Class 37, though, their performance curve was not ideal for 100mph running, but then neither is that of the 2,580bhp Class 47s — and look at the volume of high-speed mileage that class accumulates.

Table 3: Bristol Temple Meads-Birmingham New Street

Train: 13.25 Weston-super-Mare to York
Locomotive: No 37197
Load: nine Mk 1s, 322 tons net, 340 tons gross

Dist		Actual	Speeds
miles		m s	mph
00.00	Bristol Temple Meads	00.00	—
0.71	DR Days Bridge Jct	2.16	26
1.62	Stapleton Road	3.51	44½
3.70	Horfield	7.11	32
4.80	Filton Jct	8.48	46½
5.86	Bristol Parkway	10.45	—
1.20	Winterbourne	3.19	47½
3.30	Coalpit Heath	4.52	53½
4.61	Westerleigh Jct	6.59	28½*
12.77	Charfield	14.35	86½
22.55	Frocester	21.21	82½
		Sigs 1½mins	
25.96	Standish Hct	28.39	44½
28.96	NAAS	31.42	67½
34.29	Gloucester	37.10	—
1.01	Barnwood Jct	2.46	37
4.52	Churchdown	5.51	55/57½
6.55	Cheltenham	9.47	—
3.80	Cleeve	4.59	70
7.25	Ashchurch	7.32	83½/84
17.96	Abbotswood Jct	15.31	74½
26.49	Droitwich Road	22.00	79½
31.36	Bromsgrove	25.47	71½
33.40	Blackwell	29.38	18½
34.90	Barnt Green	34.51	50
38.59	Northfield	35.12	72½
40.00	Kings Norton	36.51	38½/55½
		sigs ¼min	
45.53	Birmingham New Street	47.36	—

* Speed restriction

Top:
The demise of steam heating made Class 37/4 a popular alternative to Class 47/4 for charters during winter months. No 37426 was turned out for a Pathfinder tour from Plymouth to South Yorkshire, seen here on the return leg passing Diggle Junction. *David N. Clough*

Above:
The old bridge over the River Ness at Inverness. No 37418 nears journey's end with the 05.55 from Wick. *David N. Clough*

It will be useful to take a look at an example of what the class could do on a high-speed main line, as it has often been used to perform on summer Saturday trains to and from Yarmouth along the East Coast line and between York and Bristol and the West Country. Although the run in Table 3 was made on a Sunday — 26 August 1984 — it was free from engineering work. Departure was 13min late waiting for a connection and the first bit of interest was the climb through the Bristol suburbs to Horfield at 1 in 75. Assuming the minimum here of 31½mph had been sustained, it would have been worth 1,290rhp; as speed was almost certainly still falling, 37197 was a little below its nominal rating.

Getting away from Parkway, a respectable 52½mph was attained on the 1 in 300 before shutting off for the turnout at Westerleigh Junction. The long descent towards Gloucester produced speeds in the mid-80s, before being interrupted by a stop for a fault with Stonehouse level crossing. Even with the help of a downhill road, a recovery to 67mph was all that proved possible in advance of the call at Gloucester. Continuing to Cheltenham, nothing better than 57mph was achieved up the 1 in 304, not as good as the progress made from Bristol Parkway, 37197 seemed to struggle to get into speed on the favourable length to the Avon bridge after Eckington and a rather cautious passage over Abbotswood Junction meant that 80mph could not be reached on the succeeding section which, although generally adverse, does include two lengths of level track totalling nearly four miles.

The ascent of the Lickey Bank was certainly interesting. Passing Stoke Works Junction at 75mph, there was probably another slight easing through Bromsgrove, followed by a rapid falling-off in speed to around the 20mph mark, at which pace the train plodded up to the summit. As this was within the continuous rating speed, it could have been sustained indefinitely. A surprisingly good recovery saw Barnt Green passed at 50mph but the power at the rail from Stoke Works had only averaged 1,190hp. Assuming full power had been applied throughout, a figure nearer 1,300rhp should have been developed. The inevitable checks outside New Street station probably cost about 1min, giving a net time of 46½min from Cheltenham, a fair conclusion to an unremarkable run. Even allowing for 37197 being a bit down on power, the inability to top 79mph after Abbotswood Junction shows why the class, as-built, were not wholly suited to very high-speed duties.

Before moving to Scotland, and to demonstrate how good a Class 37 can be, Table 4 sets out part of a railtour from Bolton to Longannet. Now railtours are often not the best trains from the performance viewpoint. Motive power, loadings and routes may conspire to produce indifferent running. The example shown here was an exception, with March-based 37109 being drafted into the area by virtue of its operable steam boiler. A strong northerly wind blew for most of the day, though this offered neither help nor hindrance between Manchester and Leeds. Starting from Manchester Victoria, the train had to climb Miles Platting Bank, mainly at 1 in 59/47, and it was only on the easier part at the top that a slight easing was needed to avoid exceeding the 20mph restriction over the junction with the Calder Valley line. Even then the railway continues to rise, with the 1 in 135 from Clayton Bridge steepening to 1 in 100 beyond Droylesden as far as OAGB Junction. Having topped the 50mph mark, speed fell back to 48½mph, then 45½mph, before a final peak of 48mph on the run into Stalybridge.

Table 4: Manchester Victoria-Leeds
Train: Bolton-Longannet charter
Locomotive: No 37109
Load: 10 Mk 1s, 364 tons net, 385 tons gross

Dist		Actual	Speeds
miles		m s	mph
00.00	Manchester Victoria	00.00	—
1.40	Platting	4.16	24*
3.27	Clayton Bridge	7.04	51½
6.11	Oagb Jct	10.37	45½/48
7.81	Stalybridge	14.29	—
2.64	Mossley	5.22	40
4.98	Greenfield	8.29	44
6.00	Saddleworth	10.01	45½/46½
6.89	Diggle Jct	11.13	45½*/53½
10.84	Marsden	15.51	45*
13.44	Slaithwaite	18.13	77½
		tsr	45*
16.15	Longwood	21.12	65/69
17.91	Huddersfield	23.47	—
2.72	Bradley Jct	3.55	67 brakes/52
5.00	Mirfield	6.22	59/69
6.52	Thornhill LNW Jct	8.02	45*
8.05	Dewsbury	9.52	52
		sigs	20/51
12.59	Morley	17.26	32½/74
		sigs 1½min	
17.16	Leeds	26.42	—

* Speed restriction

Top:
On Wednesdays the test stock underwent maintenance and so trial trips on that day were made as pilot to 1D27, the 11.16 Crewe to Holyhead. The 14.21 return Holyhead to Cardiff is captured near Bagilt, Clwyd, during October 1986 with a refurbished Class 37 double-heading with a Class 47. *D. I. Rapson*

Above:
With Birdswood in the background, No 37430 hurries towards Weaver Junction at the head of the 17.14 Liverpool Lime Street to Cardiff, one of two diagrams on which the class substituted for Sprinters during the 1988 summer timetable. The date was 21 May. *David N. Clough*

Once out of Stalybridge Tunnel, the route rises at 1 in 125/175/125 to its first summit at Diggle, on which stretch a gradual acceleration to the mid-40s was achieved. The rate at Diggle was governed by the prevailing 45mph limit on the curve into Standedge Tunnel. This climb was very little inferior to what a Class 40 would achieve and reaching 44mph on the 1 in 125 was worth 1,400rhp. Now this is a very high figure, being 8% over rating. It was no freak, though, for later in the day, values of the same order were produced in other locations. On the level track in the tunnel a maximum of 53½mph was noted, followed by the descent to Huddersfield, taken largely without power. The timing for a Class 46 on nine bogies was 23min, start to stop, so for 37109 to have taken only 23min 47sec, with a coach more and slowing for trackwork to contend with, shows its merit.

With the route continuing downhill as far as Thornhill LNW Junction, the first 2¾ miles at 1 in 101/147, there is no difficulty restarting from Huddersfield. A liberal interpretation of the 45mph limit round the curves between the junctions at Heaton Lodge enabled a near 70mph maximum before taking the turnout at Thornhill. A recovery to 52mph was very good on the rising 1 in 223/193 past Dewsbury before signals ruined the rest of the pull up to Morley Tunnel. A spirited romp down the hill towards Leeds was rewarded with a further signal check. North of York the train ran slow line to Northallerton, so performance on the level could not be assessed. On the return, though, following an unscheduled stop at Lancaster to relight the tail lamp, speed was gradually worked up to almost 80mph on the level after Garstang. All in all, a first class effort.

Although the Scottish Region had Class 37s on its books from the 1960s, it was not until the start of the 1980s that the type was drafted on to regular passenger work, firstly on the West Highland line, then north of Inverness. Whilst the work of the Eastfield allocation often fell below expectations, the quality of that put in by the small stud at Inverness has aroused interest. Two recorders in particular, Messrs Griffin and Holden, made quite a study of running on the Far North line during the first few years of Class 37 operation there and Table 5 sets out the results of their efforts, with additional data provided by Mr M. D. Robertson. Gradually a pattern emerged, showing a steadily rising trend in the horsepower being produced. Clearly the horsepower figures of, for example, No 37114 were remarkable, well above the 1,300 value one might expect. One commentator has tried to explain these in terms of gradients to those normally quoted, but this does not explain why the values rose over the period reviewed here. A suggestion of uprating has been refuted by depot management; indeed, available power is used only intermittently, especially on the Lochalsh road, and fuel dilution, due to engines running cold, was a problem with Class 37/0 examples.

Table 5: Power Outputs for Inverness-based Class 37/0s
(Figures quoted in rail horsepower)

Locomotive Nos	1982	1983	1984	1985
37025	—	1,195	1,405	1,410
37035	1,305	1,285	1,200	1,300
37114	1,290	—	1,485	1,270
37260	1,180	1,200	1,295	1,280
37261	—	—	1,315	1,345
37262	1,235	1,400	1,345	1,425
37264	—	—	1,420	1,425
Average	1,250	1,270	1,355	1,350
No of runs	5	5	14	24

The shape of the Far North route gradient profile and the placing of its intermediate stations, means the southbound journey offers the greater interest from the performance viewpoint. Table 6 illustrates a typical trip with a Class 37/4. The first section of the run with the combined Wick and Thurso portions shows the work done on the climb to County March, followed by the remainder of the trip from Brora. The main log was recorded by Mr Griffin, added to it are parts from a journey with No 37114 to illustrate differences in performance.

Table 6: Georgemas Junction-Inverness

Date: 11 May 1987			25 May 1984		
Train: 12.00 Wick-Inverness			18.00 Wick-Inverness		
Locomotive: No 37417			No 37114+6		
Load (tons): six coaches, 200 tare, 204 gross			six coaches, 205 tare, 220 gross		

Dist		Actual	Speeds	Actual	Speeds
miles		m s	mph	m s	mph
00.00	Georgemas Jct	00.00	—	00.00	—
1.49	Halkirk	3.05	59/tsr 21/55	2.17	51/54
4.24	Scotscalder	7.17	45*/42/55	5.13	23/59
13.24	Altnabreac	18.20	45/50	15.27	—/55
17.49	County March	23.56	45/52	5.25	54½
21.40	Forsinard	29.03	—		
00.00	Brora	00.00	—	00.00	—
4.37	Dunrobin	6.38	58 /max/—	6.35	49½/53½
5.25	The Mound	4.55	53/66		
9.27	Rogart	10.22	20*	00.00	—
13.50	Acheilidh	6.52	41½	6.02	52½
16.85	Lairg Summit	21.20	44/46	9.37	55/62½
19.26	Lairg	25.45	—	12.59	—
5.53	Invershin	8.28	57/29*		
5.97	Culrain	9.48	—		
3.09	Ardgay	4.59	59/—		
8.22	Edderton	9.54	73/28/70		
13.56	Tain	16.25	—		
3.64	Fearn	5.42	59/—		
1.41	Nigg	2.25	57/66		
5.75	Delny	6.42	43*/66		
9.24	Invergordon	11.15	—		
2.85	Alness	3.56	57/—		
3.61	Evanton	4.36	68/70		
5.70	Foulis	6.20	68/70		
9.87	Dingwall	12.21	—		
2.45	Conon	3.53	53		
5.70	Muir of Ord	8.12	—		
7.18	Beauly	3.59	55/70		
11.43	Clachnaharry	14.35	10*		
13.00	Inverness	*(.)	—		

* Speed restriction

Although there are a couple of short dips, the 17½ miles from Georgemas Junction to County March are uphill and as steep is 1 in 60 in places. Scotscalder and Altnabreac are both request halts (a fairly common feature on the line) and so the schedule has to allow for this. Since No 37417 did not take many of the request stops, including section times becomes superfluous and early arrivals at other intermediate points was the rule. The ETS was in use throughout the 1987 trip and could have been taking about 75hp away from traction. With gradients fluctuating between 1 in 60/80/100 on the three miles to County March, a settled speed was not possible; the variability between the three runs is, however, still marked.

The train has the chance to get into its stride after Brora before tackling 1½ miles at 1 in 60 to Dunrobin Castle, where the request stop was made. Without calling at Rogart, No 37417 got a better start at the seven miles, averaging 1 in 86, to Lairg summit. What it is not generally appreciated is that south of MP 70 the line speed drops from 60 to 45mph and this probably helps explain the fall in speed over the last ½ mile of the climb, rather than any inaccuracy in the gradient. The table shows how speeds fluctuated with gradient and a probable slight easing for the 45mph limit. Horsepower calculations by Mr Griffin for his log confirm this, with an average 1,205rhp overall, but slightly less, at 1,195, for the last two miles. When ETS demands are added, around 1,300rhp would be the equivalent figure. No 37114's effort stands well above the work of No 37417 and was worth 1,580rhp at 52½mph on the 1 in 80. During October 1987 Mr Griffin recorded a number of climbs and the level of power output was generally consistent within the 1,300 to 1,350rhp range, quite normal for Class 37/4.

After completing the descent from Lairg summit at Culrain, the railway has no sustained gradient to impede the running seriously. Generally speaking, there is a series of humps, but their impact on speed is small. Permanent limits are more of a handicap, though speeds in the 70s are common. The revised control system and lower gearing help drivers of Class 37/4s to get away quickly from stops. The rapid cycling from 'off' to 'full' power must prove very demanding on the power units, though no figures are available to compare casualty and maintenance statistics with other examples of the type.

Inverness depot has been very satisfied with its life-extended Class 37s, which have proved trouble-free and reliable. This was important in view of the high availability called for during the summer timetable, with the extra Oban service, when six of the eight locomotives were needed just for the passenger traffic. Very little time was available for maintenance and there was no margin for contingencies if a machine had to go to works for repair or to Craigentinny for tyre turning. That the service was maintained, with only occasional calls on Class 37/0, was a testimony to the design and the way it was maintained.

Below:
Earlier the same day, 21 May 1988, No 37426 was on the other diagram, which involved two trips to Manchester. This picture was taken at Leebotwood, south of Shrewsbury, on the 10.00 from Piccadilly to Cardiff. *David N. Clough*

Finally, late delivery of, and subsequent problems with, sufficient Class 155 Super Sprinters caused two of their diagrams from Cardiff to Liverpool and Manchester to be given over to Class 37/4s during the summer 1988 timetable. When Class 155 was temporarily withdrawn from traffic in December 1988, recourse was again made to Class 37/4 motive power and by February the Cardiff to Rhyl diagram had been added to those previously worked. Table 7 looks at how the locomotives fared on Sprinter timings, particularly as the latter were much vaunted as being faster than those timings previously applied.

Table 7: Liverpool Lime Street-Crewe
Train: 09.15 Liverpool Lime Street-Cardiff (25 June 1988)
Locomotive: No 37429
Load: four Mk 2s, 130 tons tare, 135 tons gross

Dist		Sched	Actual	Speeds
miles	Liverpool	min	m s	mph
00.00	Lime Street	0	00.00	—
1.35	Edge Hill	4	3.56	29½
4.60	West Allerton	?	8.08	83½
6.41	Speke Jct	10	9.39	68/81
10.60	Ditton Jct	13½	12.55	brakes
13.10	Runcorn	16	15.48	—
1.25	Halton Jct	2½	2.23	49
3.25	Sutton Weaver	—	4.21	72½
5.99	Weaver Jct	6½	6.42	66½
8.00	Acton Bridge	—	8.20	77/77½
10.70	Hartford	11	11.07	—
8.50	Coppenhall	(2)	9.15	79½
11.80	Crewe	13½	13.33	—

The usual load for these services was four Mk 2 vehicles, incidentally offering a better standard of accommodation, as well as more seats, than a Class 155. No 37429 did not prove to be the best performer timed on these duties, but this perhaps offers a better example of the ordinary, rather than the exceptional. A feature common to these substitutions was the willingness of the drivers to run at speeds in excess of the 80mph maximum permitted for the class. No 37429 was not pushed up the steep climb from Liverpool, possibly due to a preceding empty stock working. A brisk acceleration followed, then a reduction through the curves at Speke Junction, with another run up to 80mph before easing for the run into Runcorn.

Getting away from Runcorn on a 1 in 115 proved no difficulty, with 49mph attained by Halton Junction. Power was cut off on the downgrade after Sutton Weaver and this coasting meant Weaver Junction was passed a little below the permitted limit. Recovery to 77mph against the 1 in 330 to Acton Bridge was good and there was little further acceleration before braking commenced for the Hartford call. With an initial mile at 1 in 380 down, good progress was made towards Winsford Junction, which continued up the two miles of 1 in 410 before that point. It was here that the brakes went on for a temporary speed restriction through Winsford station. Facing five miles of rising track towards the site of Coppenhall Junction before the line levels out, the continued use of full power failed to quite produce an 80mph maximum before the usual cautious approach to Crewe, where use of Platform 11, on the down side, involved crossing the station throat. Final arrival was on time.

On the continuation from Crewe the Class 37/4 had no difficulty in maintaining sectional timings. A few minutes' deficit was accumulated by Cwmbran but this was entirely due to the volume of passengers and the consequential time spent at stations. The extra seating offered by a four-coach rake over a two-car Class 155 was of benefit.

Chapter 6

Current Duties

No other type of BR diesel locomotive can lay claim to the geographical supremacy of Class 37. Each day, members of the class can be found literally anywhere between Cornwall and Caithness. By the late autumn of 1989, sectorisation had become a prime factor in the utilisation of the entire fleet. The 304 locomotives comprising the class are to be found allocated to nine different depots (as at December 1989), and their duties fall into three basic Sector categories viz: Departmental (25 locomotives), Provincial (4) and Freight (275).

PROVINCIAL

By far the largest allocation is that of Cardiff Canton (CF) depot, where 95 locomotives are maintained, including all four of the Provincial batch. Hence, Cardiff is the only depot to have engines from each of the three categories mentioned above. Diagrammed passenger duties for the electric train heating variety (sub-class 37/4) cover both the Cambrian line (Shrewsbury to Aberystwyth) and the North and West route (Cardiff to Liverpool and Manchester Piccadilly). During November 1989, Cardiff lost half of its Provincial allocation (four 37/4s moving temporarily to Immingham for Departmental and Freight use during the winter months). A Nottingham-Blackpool North service took a 37/4 to the famous resort on the Lancashire coast for a brief period during the autumn of 1989, whilst the summer Cardiff-Weymouth had allowed the class access to Somerset and Dorset. A late flourish to the year saw 37/4s visit Cambridge and Carlisle.

FREIGHT

Petroleum

Use of the Class 47 for hauling heavy trains of oil tanks, and the prospect of the Class 60 arrival in the early 1990s, has meant that only 28 of the English Electric Type 3s belong to Petroleum-related pools (all statistics correct to December 1989). Though Cardiff

Below:
Railfreight Petroleum Sector paid for the refurbishment and conversion of a small fleet of Class 37/7s for traffic flows which take their motive power off Stratford depot in East London. At Ripple Lane on 2 December 1987 No 37889 stands at the head of the 14.45 to Langley, whilst No 37893 is on the 15.01 to Thame. Note the sector livery, with chevron transfers. *Paul Shannon*

Below:
Stratford also turns out pairs of Class 37s to power the Freightliner traffic on the Anglia Region. On 29 May 1987 Nos 153+008 wheel a Willesden to Felixstowe service through the East Anglian countryside near Colchester; the rear locomotive retains a Scottie emblem from its days at Eastfield. *M. J. Collins*

Centre:
The extra tractive capacity of Class 37/7 has led to them being rostered to some of the heavier duties associated with South Wales traffic. No 37717, allocated to Cardiff Canton's Metals sub-Sector, traverses the North & West line near Craven Arms on 1 April 1989 with the 06.35 Mossend New Yard to Margam. *Steve Turner*

Bottom:
Speedlink Coal has fleets of both refurbished Class 37/5s and as-built Class 37/0s for its duties. No 37680 passes Marshfield between Newport and Cardiff on its way back to South Wales, having worked a train of Cawoods coal containers to Ellesmere Port. *M. J. Collins*

Top:
On 15 January 1989 No 37131 passes Moreton, en route for Didcot coal depot, on the Down Slow line as No 50035 thunders past with the 14.15 Paddington to Oxford.
Steve Turner

Above:
Not all the current work of the class is on trainload services. No 37062, withdrawn early in 1989 following collision damage at Warrington, powers the trip freight from Long Marston to Worcester along the branch to Honeybourne on 9 February 1988.
Steve Turner

Canton has the largest fleet (nine locomotives), Eastfield and Stratford depots follow close behind, having eight apiece. Cardiff's Petroleum engines (seven 37/0s and two 37/3s) include the popular No 37350 (originally D6700, the pioneer of the class) which sports a dark green livery, closely resembling that carried during the 1960s. Their rosters involve working in multiple on tanker trains from Robeston (near Milford Haven) to destinations at Theale (near Reading) and Langley (east of Slough). Localised traffic within South Wales originates at Llandarcy (between Swansea and Neath), with nearby Briton Ferry acting as a staging point for traffic going onwards to Margam, Aberthaw and Grangetown.

Whilst locomotives are based at Eastfield depot (Glasgow), their Petroleum duties in the south of Scotland are centred upon Grangemouth, near Falkirk. From here services run to Dalston (Cumbria), Tyne Yard and Jarrow in the Northeast and to such Scottish destinations as Bishopbriggs (Glasgow), Leith, Paisley, Prestwick and Riccarton

(Kilmarnock). Chemical traffic to Haverton Hill and Larbert also falls within the scope of Eastfield's Class 37 fleet, five of which are 37/0 locomotives. In November 1989, two 37/7s (37707/8) arrived from Immingham, in readiness for a new flow of traffic to Inverness, via the steeply-graded Highland main line.

The remaining 11 Petroleum 37s are diagrammed to work from Stratford depot in East London (eight members of sub-Class 37/7), and from Immingham (Humberside). During the latter part of 1989, two of Stratford's allocation actually belonged to an Immingham-based pool. Oil trains from Ripple Lane (Barking) take Stratford's machines to Kilnhurst (near Mexborough, South Yorkshire), Micheldever (on the Southern Region's main line from Basingstoke to Southampton) and Four Ashes near Wolverhampton, as well as a variety of locations within the Home Counties. Two of the three 37s acquired by Immingham in November 1989 belonged to the Stanlow fleet, and included a Class 37/4 locomotive for use on the weekly Stanlow-Aberystwyth service.

Metals
No fewer than 95 Class 37 locomotives belong to the Metals sub-Sector, including the entire Thornaby (Teesside) allocation of the class, which totalled 46 as at December 1989. The 37/5 variants (37501-37521 and 37667/8) see work on steel traffic from the BSC plant at Lackenby (east of Middlesbrough) to Corby, Workington, Etruria (Stoke-on-Trent) and Wolverhampton. Their other steel-related diagrams encompass journeys to Carlisle, Mossend, Leith, Tinsley, Redmire, Scunthorpe, the West Midlands and Cardiff. Nearly two dozen 37/0s complement the above, and work additionally to locations in the Northwest (at Glazebrook and Warrington), Scotland (Stranraer) and South Wales. Motherwell's 18 Metals engines are largely employed on the extensive ore train workings between British Steel's Ravenscraig plant and the Hunterston Ore complex in Ayrshire. Nevertheless, they also have diagrams involving trips to Tyne Yard and to Washwood Heath (Birmingham). Immingham depot has a small contingent (six) of Class 37s similarly deployed on ore train operation from the adjacent dock to Santon (Scunthorpe).

On the Western Region, Cardiff's 25 Metals locomotives have much of their work centred upon the steelworks in and around Newport, and at Tidal Yard, Cardiff. Again the transportation of ore features largely in South Wales, with 37/7s being employed daily on the heavy ore traffic between Port Talbot docks and BSC Llanwern, utilising BSC-owned PTA bogie tippler wagons. All six of the 37/9 sub-class (37901-37906) are based at Canton depot and regularly journey northwards to Dee Marsh (Shotton Steelworks, Clwyd) with hot rolled coil for finishing. They return with similar loads from

Below left:
No 37062 again, this time towing London Regional Transport battery locomotives
Nos L45 and L44. The train is the 11.56 West Ruislip to Crewe Works, approaching
Leamington Spa on 30 April 1988. *Steve Turner*

Above:
Cambrian line passenger services will soon be one of only two routes on which the
Provincial Sector will retain locomotive-and-stock formations. Since this photograph
was taken on 21 May 1988 the manual signalling has been replaced by RETB. The
signalman at Welshpool has just exchanged the single line token with the driver of
No 37429+427 on the 09.40 Euston to Aberystwyth. *David N. Clough*

Below:
With the demise of Class 25, South Wales-based Class 37/0s took over their duties on the
Cambrian. They remained in use on summer Saturdays until ScotRail could release
sufficient Class 37/4s from May 1989. On 11 June 1988 Nos 37197+079 approach
Welshpool with the 15.05 Pwhelli to Euston. *D. I. Rapson*

Below:
Canton's stud of Class 37/4s have seen a variety of use away from the Cambrian. Among these have been visits to Weymouth. No 37427 was used on 16 April 1988 as motive power for an additional service from Cardiff. *Steve Turner*

Right:
A diesel weekend on the Severn Valley Railway on 7 May 1988 found No 37427 at Bewdley. *D. I. Rapson*

Below right:
Speedlink Distribution replaced Laira's Class 37/0s with Class 37/5s in 1987. On 29 September of that year Nos 37671 and 37675 stand in Par station on old-style clayhood wagons. *D. I. Rapson*

Crewe, carrying traffic that originated at Ravenscraig, via Mossend Yard. With a depot allocation of 95 Class 37s, Cardiff has by far the largest percentage of the type on its books. Recently refurbished sub-Classes 37/5 and 37/7 both feature largely in the daily workforce. Steel workings take the 37/7s into North Wales and Greater Manchester, and to the West Midlands (Brierley Hill and Round Oak), Swindon Cocklebury and to West Wales (to the Trostre and Velindre plants, between Llanelli and Swansea).

Coal

Fifty Class 37 locomotives belong to the Coal sub-Sector, most of them (44) in pools FQCK, FHBK and FEKK at Cardiff Canton. The remaining half-dozen are to be found at Eastfield in the Lothians fleet (FEPE) which they share with a batch of Class 26 types. Three of the Scottish-based locomotives are 37/3 examples for use on the

Ayr-Ravenstruther workings (Ravenstruther being an opencast coal disposal point north of Carstairs). The principal flow of opencast coal to Ayr Harbour, however, is from Knockshinnoch disposal point, near New Cumnock.

The Cardiff allocation may be further dissected into three distinct categories: DCN Coal (14 locomotives), Trainload Coal (10) and Aberthaw Coal duties (20). The latter pool is made up entirely of 37/7 machines rostered on merry-go-round hopper trains to the power station located west of Barry, the train crew centre for such operations. The pattern of MGR workings varies weekly, depending upon the supply from the few remaining pits in South Wales. Following colliery closures in the late summer of 1989, only six pits remain in the whole of South Wales. Containerised coal traffic is moved from West Glamorgan and Dyfed to Ellesmere Port (for shipment to Northern Ireland), being hauled throughout by Class 37s, and to Swansea Docks.

Speedlink coal traffic links collieries with over 30 concentration depots around the country. Thus, Cardiff's 37/0 engines are diagrammed to operate to such locations as Neasden, Eastleigh, Didcot, West Drayton, Washwood Heath, Preston, Birkenhead, Gobowen, Cambridge, Ipswich, Doncaster, Millerhill, Toton and Yeovil.

Below:
No 37095 leaves a truncated Millerhill Yard with a Thrislington to Gartcosh service on 5 May 1987. *Tom Noble*

Bottom:
When insufficient funds were available for full refurbishment, Class 37s in need of classified repair were given an Intermediate but fitted with regeared bogies; this gave a higher tractive effort at low speed. Locomotives treated in this way were renumbered into the range starting with No 37350 and classified Class 37/3. In pouring rain on 2 September 1988, No 37379 shunts the permanent way depot at Rutherglen, Glasgow. *David N. Clough*

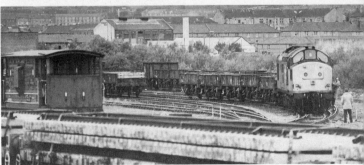

Top:
Tank traffic between Grangemouth and Bishopbriggs continue to produce Class 37/0s in multiple. By 27 June 1988, when this illustration was taken, No 37035 had moved to Eastfield from Inverness and acquired a bodyside Scottie motif in place of a Highland stag; the second engine is No 37118. *Tom Noble*

Above:
Most of the freights over the Highland line are rostered for Class 37. In this view, taken on 24 May 1988, No 37109 passes Dalnacardoch at the head of the 13.40 Inverness to Millerhill. *D. I. Rapson*

Below:
Not much passenger work is now diagrammed for the class in Scotland, quite a contrast from the start of 1989. A regular tour train, the 'Royal Scotsman' departs Edinburgh Waverley for Oban behind No 37411 on 7 June 1988. *Tom Noble*

Top:
Overhead line equipment indicates progress with East Coast electrification in the vicinity of Dunbar. No 37309, renumbered on 1 February 1989 to No 37274 to avoid confusion with the new Class 37/3 sub-class, shows clearly the Coal sub-Sector livery, with its black and yellow transfers. The working is a Gartcosh to Healey Mills coal empties, photographed on 22 August 1988. *Tom Noble*

Above:
Inter-Regional workings see quite a lot of Class 37 activity along the former Midland line northeast out of Birmingham. On 17 March 1989 No 37054 is found at Water Orton with the 08.42 Wolverhampton Steel Terminal to Scunthorpe in tow. *Steve Turner*

Above:
Class 37 under repair. Scheduled maintenance above an A exam is invariably carried out by the home depot. In this case, Thornaby takes care of No 37504 during April 1988.
C. R. Holland

Below:
The Tinsley fleet, allocated to the Construction sub-Sector, have a regular working along the North Wales coast, hauling the Penmaenmawr to Washwood Heath service. On 10 June 1988 Nos 37688+671 pass beneath one of Sandycroft's signals on the return empties. *D. I. Rapson*

Distribution

This particular Sector was formed in the autumn of 1988 by the merger of Railfreight Speedlink and Freightliners Limited. Some 69 Class 37s belong to Distribution pools, 45 of them at Tinsley depot in South Yorkshire and the remaining 24 in Scotland (11 at Eastfield and 13 at Inverness). Railfreight's wagonload business is extremely varied, and the 'Syphons' (as the 37s are nicknamed) enjoy a similarly wide range of use, being rostered to Speedlink and Freightliner traffic throughout the country. Thus, a Tinsley Class 37 may be seen daily at such extremities of the system as Aberdeen (Guild Street) and Warminster, Inverness and Boston or Carmarthen and Stranraer.

Much of their work on Freightliner traffic may be witnessed in East Anglia, where they venture to Felixstowe and Parkeston terminals, and on trains to and from Coatbridge and Glasgow.

Construction

Whilst as many as 33 members of the class belong to Construction-related pools, their duties fall into less than half a dozen particular spheres. Laira depot, in Plymouth, has a total Class 37 allocation of just nine, and all find use on china clay traffic originating in Cornwall. The inauguration of a new twice-weekly service from Burngullow (near St Austell) to Irvine in southwest Scotland during March 1989 has led to Laira's machines spreading their wings, as a pair of 37/5s hauls the tanks throughout.

Another tiny pool (just three 37/3 locomotives) belongs to Motherwell depot, purely for the operation of a daily cement train running between the Ribblesdale plant at Clitheroe, near Blackburn and Gunnie (Coatbridge).

Stratford's five Class 37s (four 37/0 and a single 37/3) for aggregates traffic (Pool AGS) involve themselves between Ipswich and Claydon or Leiston, on the Middleton Towers 'sand' branch (King's Lynn) and on trains from March to Kennett, Claydon, Barham or Norwich Trowse. Finally, Tinsley has amongst its depot fleet, 16 EE Type 3s (three of sub-Class 37/4 and the remainder 37/5s) principally for use on the heavy stone traffic emanating within the Peak District of Derbyshire, and centred primarily upon Buxton. A recent development, involving the use of privately-owned wagons, has seen pairs of Class 37/5 types operating along the North Wales coast line (Penmaenmawr to Ashburys, Manchester) and between Peak Forest and Bletchley.

DEPARTMENTAL

The 25 Class 37s so far not accounted for belong to various British Rail Departmental pools. Such locomotives are to receive all-over grey with yellow band livery, which does little to enhance their appearance. 37025, an Eastfield engine, was the first to be so painted, having been the initial recipient of the large-logo blue livery back in December 1983. Departmental-allocated 37s belong to Cardiff Canton (13), Eastfield (five), Immingham (five) and Stratford (two), the most noteworthy inclusions being 37407/8/26 transferred in to Immingham's squad during the winter months, having enjoyed lengthy use on passenger turns between Cardiff and the Northwest and on the Cambrian lines.

Summary of Class 37 allocations by sub-Sector
(Correct to 21 January 1991)

Cardiff Canton (CF)

DCWA	23	Departmental RCE Western
FMHK	20	Railfreight Metals
FPEK	13	Railfreight Petroleum, South Wales
FMAK	5	Railfreight Metals
FQCK	10	Railfreight Distribution (Network Coal)
FHBK	8	Railfreight Coal, Trainload
FEKK	20	Railfreight Coal, Trainload, Aberthaw

Eastfield (ED)

DCHA	10	Departmental RCE ScotRail
FDTE	11	Railfreight Distribution
FPAE	9	Railfreight Petroleum & Chemicals
FDUE	6	Railfreight Distribution
FEPE	9	Railfreight Coal, Scotland

Immingham (IM)

DCEA	6	Departmental RCE Eastern
FPFR	7	Railfreight Petroleum, North Thames, Ripple Lane
FABI	21	Railfreight Construction
FMYI	4	Railfreight Metals

Thornaby (TE)

FMTY	38	Railfreight Metals
FALY	7	Railfreight Construction, Cement
FCTY	6	Railfreight Distribution (Chemicals)
FPBC	5	Railfreight Petroleum, Stanlow

Tinsley (TI)

FDET	30	Railfreight Distribution

Motherwell (ML)

FMGM	23	Railfreight Metals, Hunterston

Laira (LA)

FCLL	9	Railfreight Distribution, China Clay, St Blazey

Stratford (SF)

DCAA	2	Departmental RCE Anglia

Other Sectors

FDYX	1	Railfreight Distribution, stored (37096)
FXXA	2	Railfreight General (37197 & 37258 su)

Sub-Sector summary by allocation of Class 37 locomotives

Departmental	41
Freight (Chemicals)	15
Freight (Coal)	47
Freight (Construction)	28
Freight (Distribution)	47
Freight (Metals)	90
Freight (Petroleum)	34
General	3
Total	305

Top:
Most of the work of Tinsley's Class 37/5s is associated with Peak District stone output. Nos 37681+678 shunt at Peak Forest. *Paul Shannon*

Centre:
Although Nos 37681+682 are bathed in brilliant sunshine, the clouds appear menacing as the machines discharge their load of crushed stone from Tunstead at Collyhurst on 4 August 1987. *David N. Clough*

Above:
During the early 1980s the class took over responsibility for the cement flows from Roes Newydd and Horrocksford to Gunnie. On 16 February 1987 Nos 37102+050 pass Roes Newydd North Fork with the 14.00 down. *D. I. Rapson*

Chapter 7

Class 37 from the Footplate

Most enthusiasts would leap at the opportunity to travel in the cab of a locomotive. These days, this privilege is granted only very rarely by BR, as it involves the visitor being accompanied by a traction inspector, who has more important duties to perform. When a cab pass is provided, however, it is sensible to make the most of it. For this reason the best trains to ride are freights, the working of which cannot be studied in the same way as a passenger train. After all, it is fairly easy to visualise what is going on in the cab of a passenger train, particularly if the passenger is in a DMU compartment just behind the driver. In the era of the block train, commercial requirements bring a need for punctuality and intensive utilisation of resources. For these reasons, therefore, it was decided to examine two block workings at first hand. The two selected were to give the reader examples of both as-built and life-extended locomotives. In the case of the latter it was sensible to see how the Class 37/9s were expected to perform on freights which represent the heaviest loads allocated to any Class 37. Grateful thanks go to the Scottish and Western Regions for providing the footplate facilities.

Ravenscraig to Hunterston
As noted earlier in this book, the BSC traffic centred on the Ravenscraig steelworks near Motherwell has a dedicated fleet of Class 37/0 locomotives to meet its needs. The

Below:
Driving position of a Class 37/4. To the left are the locomotive air brake (upper) and train brake (lower) handles. Above the former is the control knob for the driver's windscreen wiper. The top two dials are speedometer and ammeter, the lower three are brake pipe pressure, vacuum, and brake cylinder pressure, with the main reservoir gauge to the right. At the right side of the kneehole position is the horn control. To the right are the master control switch and power control handle. Above the latter, the blanking plate denotes where slow speed control equipment would be installed. The vane display above this is the automatic warning system unit, with cancel button immediately to its left. *S. R. Griffin*

operation of both the iron ore and coal, brought in through the deep-water port at Hunterston on the Clyde estuary near to Largs, is in trainloads formed for haulage by two locomotives in multiple; driver-only operation applies. The normal practice is for five pairs of Class 37/0 to work out of Motherwell depot, to which they are allocated, whilst another two pairs are manned by Polmadie men for work-sharing purposes. Whilst the pattern of diagramming does change to meet customer and operating requirements, in 1988 this traffic was on a three-shift, 24-hour-day cycle, Monday to Friday, with two turns on a Saturday. Train formations are either 21 PTA wagons for iron ore or 38 HAA wagons for coal. This latter was reduced in 1987 from 46 vehicles to bring the gross tonnage below 2,000 so that a bank engine was not needed from Mossend Yard up to the steelworks.

Freight trains are timetabled in the same way as are passenger services but, as they do not operate to a public schedule, they can run at times to meet the needs of the traffic and available paths on the railway. Thus it was on 4 December 1987 that Nos 37320+324, the two locomotives for 6T75, left Motherwell depot, in the care of Driver J. Rhoden; Traction Inspector J. McGuinness was also present. The time was 10.13, some 15 minutes early, and the pair proceeded to Ravenscraig No 2 Sidings to collect 21 PTAs which were to be taken to Hunterston for loading; the train weight was given as 723 tonnes.

Ravenscraig Steelworks is situated on the Holytown loop, which leaves the West Coast main line at Law Junction, between Carstairs and Motherwell, and rejoins it at Uddingston. Signalling is under the control of Motherwell power signalbox. The site occupies land on both sides of the railway, No 2 being on the Up side. Different sidings are used for the different traffic flows, raw materials, such as iron ore and coal, finished steel etc. Running straight into the No 2 Sidings and coupling on to the wagons, as soon as the brake test had been done the train was signalled on its way at 10.29, 38 minutes early. A short burst of full power took it over the crest close to Holytown Junction (where the line from Edinburgh via Shotts converges) and then it was possible to coast virtually all the way to Glasgow. Perhaps surprisingly, as the booked path was not being followed, a clear road was given over Uddingston Junction, where the West Coast main line is joined, and similar progress ensued as far as Polmadie where a brief signal stop appeared to be due merely to Glasgow power box not being able to set the road in time, due to a large number of other movements in the vicinity.

Taking the curve away from the Glasgow Central line at Larkfield Junction, the Glasgow to Ayr route was gained at Shields Junction, just to the east of the traction depot. The next section of the journey was along a very busy artery which, as far as Paisley, carries the EMU services on the South Clyde routes, in addition to those serving Ayr, Largs and Ardrossan Pier. With an EMU literally every few minutes, it is no easy task to path a heavy freight train, such as would be the case on the return run from Hunterston. The combination of reduced train speed (for braking reasons) and slower acceleration, mean there is quite a speed difference between the EMU and the freight services. With two Class 37s on only 723 tonnes, this was less of a problem on this outward trip.

With moderate gradients the train cruised along at its permitted 50mph maximum speed until a signal stop at Kilwinning Junction was enforced to allow an Up Ayr EMU to call at the station and depart. Paisley power box was, however, on its toes, as the EMU had no sooner cleared than the road was reset and 6T75 allowed to restart and head down the Largs branch. At Stewerston the train was looped for 38 minutes as Hunterston still had an ore train being loaded and there was a wait until this was clear of the terminal; it was in fact passed near Ardrossan South Beach, hauled by another of Motherwell's pairs of Class 37s. The loop at Stewerston can only accommodate 21 PTAs plus two locomotives, and this is the limiting factor on the size of the ore trains on this route. Although there are upper and lower termini at Hunterston, generally only the former is used. Entering the sidings, the train proceeded at the stipulated 5mph to the opposite end of the site so that the wagons could be positioned under the loading point. Positioning is very important as the vehicles are moved automatically through the loader and the first wagon has to be in exactly the right place; no shunting locomotives are employed.

Slip working is employed for train loading. This means that the set brought in by the locomotives are left for loading whilst the locomotives take out a loaded rake brought in

Above:
On 14 July 1988 Nos 37326+312 charge past Cardonald with the 15.26 Ravenscraig to Hunterston iron ore empties. *P. D. Shannon*

empty on the preceding train. The type of vehicles, PTAs or HAAs, is determined by Ravenscraig's needs for either ore or coal; Hunterston can load either material. Of the three other trains seen that day, two were formed of PTAs and one of HAAs. The return trip to Ravenscraig would be with 38 HAAs and final loading was still in progress as the paperwork for the train was received which gave the gross trailing tonnage as 1,938. The Class 37s made their way to couple on to the front of them. Train 6T05 set off at 13.24, over an hour early, and attained 15mph before taking the junction to run alongside the single-track Largs branch (singled during electrification, with only freight from Hunterston using the former Up line until after Ardrossan). A minimum speed at 15mph is required to ensure a run at the bank, which might not otherwise be cleared if rail conditions were poor. On the day of this trip rail conditions were fine, as was the weather generally. After its trial uprating to 2,000bhp, No 37292 was deployed for several years on these Ravenscraig to Hunterston turns. Its extra power, and tractive effort, was appreciated by drivers in getting away from Hunterston.

Unfortunately no gradient profile is available for either the Largs branch or the Rutherglen & Coatbridge line, so it was not possible to judge accurately the work of the locomotives over these sections. After a signal stop outside Saltcoats for an EMU from Ardrossan Pier, followed by a check approaching Kilwinning for the same reason, the motive power ran comfortably at, or just above, the 45mph maximum speed permitted for the train. Once the initial acceleration was completed after Dalry the remainder of the climb at 1 in 600 past Glengarrock was taken at well below full power. Onwards to Paisley some coasting was needed to avoid excessive speed. Thus the power on hand with these workings is more than sufficient to keep them moving amidst the intensive EMU service at their top speed.

At the west end of Shields the single line turnout which leads the freight line under the main route into Glasgow Central was taken, thus avoiding a conflicting movement across the main running lines. This freight route is joined by the former railway out of the docks, known as the Burma Road (once you were in, you didn't come out, so bad was the congestion once). Most of the once-extensive railway network hereabouts has now gone and the route rejoins that followed in the down direction just before Terminus Junction. Curving round to Larkfield Junction and the West Coast line, a virtually clear road allowed full power to be used, as the remainder of the run to Ravenscraig would now be virtually all uphill.

Whereas on the outward journey, part of the route had been down the West Coast main line, this is not possible for the return leg. This is because of the ruling gradient on Bellshill Bank, beyond Uddingston, which has over two miles at 1 in 70. Two Class 37/0s with upwards of 2,000 tonnes cannot be relied upon on such a climb, though trials were made in the summer of 1987 using two Class 37/7s. Having lower gearing, extra adhesion, improved sanders and a more sophisticated control system, this sub-class has substantial advantage over a pair of standard Class 37s. Storming across the various turnouts and leaving the main line at Rutherglen East Junction the motive power charged Bellahouston Bank. Speed dropped to the mid-twenties, with a field reversion at 27mph. From the railway point of view the Rutherglen & Coatbridge line is now virtually a desert, devoid of passenger traffic and intermediate freight sidings since Carmyle Yard closed. The driver considered 22mph was the normal minimum on this climb, so to be a few mph up on this shows the two Class 37s were in good order.

Leaving the Coatbridge railway at Langloan Junction, the main line from Motherwell to Stirling and the north was gained at Whifflet and full power again was used whilst passing Mossend Yard to gather momentum for the pull up to Holytown Junction, the climb varying from 1 in 77/86/93, In fact a slight easing was needed over the junctions at Mossend North but speed fell away gradually to a minimum of 25mph. If the total tonnage had exceeded 2,000 banking assistance would have been taken over this section; on the day in question the banker would have been a Class 20. Once over the crest of the climb speed had to be kept in check for the turnout along the Down line and into Ravenscraig Number 3, the coal discharge sidings. Arrival was at 15.11 and, once released from the train, the locomotives returned to Motherwell depot for fuelling and stabling. This accomplished before 15.25, the driver had completed his shift one and a half hours early. During the week a three-shift, 24-hour pattern of operation is adopted, so Nos 37324+320 would retrace their steps in the evening.

The foregoing description makes the job seem easy; it is not always so straightforward. Firstly, the weather on the day of the journey was fine, calm and frosty. No slipping occurred, indeed no sanding was needed. Bad weather — high winds — can blow the sand off the rails, whilst high humidity can clog up the sand pipes. Poor adhesion can be a problem, particularly on the Up run leaving Hunterston. Secondly, plant or motive power breakdowns can disrupt severely the operation of the service which relies on punctuality for slick operation as can be seen from the slip working for wagon loading. If 6T75 had not been running so early there would have been no need for the wait in Stewerston loop. Thirdly, operating difficulties, such as signal or

Below:
On the day of the run described here, No 37906 stands in pouring rain at Crewe Gresty Lane, ready for departure to Cardiff Tidal Sidings. *David N. Clough*

overhead line failures, especially on the Ayr line, can hamper punctuality. It is fair to say that the run on 4 December was as near perfect as there is and it shows how efficiently and smoothly the railways can transport heavy loads with no fuss. Each HAA wagon would correspond to a single road vehicle, so 6T05 saved 38 lorries pounding along the roads out of Hunterston. BR does not have a monopoly of this work; some road haulage is used by BSC. Following the 1984-85 miners' strike, when train crews refused to work the BSC traffic, total reliance was placed with road and it has taken time to gradually wean the share of the traffic contracted to BR back to former levels.

Crewe to Newport

The background to the Class 37/9 project has already been considered. It is therefore fitting to be able to offer here an example of that sub-class's performance in its 'natural' environment, ie hauling heavy steel sub-Sector trains. By kind permission of the WR a footplate trip was made on 27 October 1987 on one of the steel coil trains which operate between Ravenscraig in Scotland and South Wales. The journey was made under ideal conditions; there was a maximum load and the weather was windy and wet throughout. This was indeed a stern test for a 1,750bhp locomotive, for the North & West line is far from an easy one over which to haul 1,410 tonnes.

6V75 arrived from the north via the independent lines to the west of Crewe station and the two Class 86 locomotives reversed the train back off the Shrewsbury line into the sidings at Gresty Lane to facilitate the traction change. The Class 37/9 No 37906 had arrived at Crewe as part of a diagram which had already seen it take a steel train from Llanwern to Dee Marsh Junction (for Shotton steelworks) before running light to take over 6V75. Driver Ecclestone of Shrewsbury was in charge, having taken over No 37906 at Shrewsbury on its run to Dee Marsh; Inspector Dennis Flood of Swindon was also present. Departing three minutes early in pouring rain, full power was not used until three minutes into the run and this did not last long before easing for a signal check approaching Nantwich. From here the route climbs to just before Whitchurch on broken gradients. A temporary speed restriction was thus unfortunate and getting away from it the driver dropped sand, through this was a preventative measure as no slipping occurred. As the climb steepened, so speed fell to a minimum of 18mph on the 1 in 115 by MP12. On the generally downhill continuation speed was kept as high as possible. This meant that only half a minute was dropped on schedule to Shrewsbury, despite suffering 5½ minutes in checks. Full power had been employed for nearly half the distance.

For enthusiasts used to riding in a coach, the footplate of a locomotive is quite a different world. To start with, there is a confined feeling, due to the reduced space. The noise is different to that experienced in a train. Unless a cab window is open the sound of the exhaust is inaudible; instead one hears turbocharger whine, or the sound of the electrical machines, such as main generator or traction motors. When travelling in No 1 end cab the radiator fan may be audible. At No 2 end, the sound of the relays in the clean air compartment may be detected. In general, a locomotive gives a harder ride than a coach, due to the extra weight on each axle. This does not make it uncomfortable, especially when seated. Class 37 has bogies which offer a steady ride which is more comfortable than most BR diesels and better than the electric classes, which can be rough riders sometimes.

A 27 minutes crew change was allowed at Shrewsbury, but the actual time taken was only five minutes and so departure was 22 minutes early. Driver A. G. Shaw of Hereford had now taken over, having travelled down by passenger train. Again, there was no rush to apply full power, the controller not being opened wide until approaching Sutton Bridge Junction. Signalling here is still of the former Great Western Railway lower quadrant pattern, a type which predominates until south of Abergavenny. Although this was a joint line with the London & North Western Railway, clearly the GWR was responsible for signalling equipment. The route is fitted with automatic warning system (AWS) apparatus: magnets fixed in the centre of the track some distance in front of each signal provide auto visual warning to the driver of the signal's aspect. The warning is on a circular display on the driver's instrument panel, whilst a bell or horn sounds to denote green or adverse aspects. Once an adverse signal is approached and the AWS warning given, the driver has a few seconds to cancel the warning, otherwise the train brakes are applied automatically.

The 12 miles to Church Stretton offered a severe test of the locomotive's capabilities, being at an average gradient of 1 in 152 but as steep as 1 in 90/100 in places. It is no exaggeration to say that the performance here was a superb demonstration of tractive capability. Despite wet rails there was no detectable slipping and No 37906 settled down to slog its way uphill at full power, the speed rising and falling with the changes of grade. It is hard to imagine that the English Electric Co designers of the D6700s in 1958/59 ever envisaged that their basic design would be diagrammed for such punishing work. Speed averaged 22½mph and Driver Shaw said the signalmen disliked these trains because they took so long to clear their sections. Without precise rolling resistance formulae for the load a really accurate estimate of the power developed is not possible. Bearing in mind, though, that the low speed would mean this element would be relatively unimportant, calculating the work done against gravity and the rolling resistance of the locomotive equates to 1,400hp. Adding about 100hp for the rolling resistance of the train gives 1,500hp at the rail. Such a figure is very high in relation to the nominal 1,750bhp at which the diesel is rated and suggests No 37906 was developing something over that amount.

It was a pleasant surprise to pass quite a number of northbound freights; most of these had Class 47 motive power. The second Class 37/9 (there were two daily diagrams from South Wales to the Northwest at the time) had been spotted stabled at Shrewsbury. Class 47/4s were in charge of the passenger traffic, the run predating the advent of Sprinters.

After suffering both signal and track repair slowings, the train was kept close to its 60mph maximum speed over the ensuing undulating course along the Welsh Marches. The train crawled into Hereford under adverse signals and was held on the through road for a passenger train to clear Tram Inn. Although booked a second crew change, Driver Shaw continued. Departure from Hereford was 24 minutes early in pouring rain and there was a slight slip as No 37906 picked up speed; no sand was used, or needed, as correction was immediate. Speed had attained 34½mph before the rising grades took their toll and there was a minimum of 17½ on the 1 in 104 over the minor summit before Tram Inn. Over 3 minutes of coasting past Pontrilas meant that the 6¼ mile long Llanvihangel Bank at 1 in 100 was begun in fine style. Notwithstanding this, the summit was only cleared at 17½mph. Skilful handling of the locomotive avoided excessive speed on the switchback course forward to the Usk bridge outside Newport. The rapid fall in speed which had accompanied the two previous uphill lengths after Hereford was repeated on the 1 in 104 past Pontypool Road, but that marked the end of the hard work for No 37906. Still running 24 minutes early, it was not surprising there was a slight signal check approaching Newport.

Having traversed the North & West line quite a few times on passenger workings, it was quite a contrast to do so on a heavy freight. This is because of the speed differential. From Church Stretton to Hereford the gradients allow a rate of progress as good as a train calling at the intermediate stations but on the banks the lower power to weight ratio results in the sensation of being able to walk faster! This is not the locomotive's fault, it is slogging away at its limit of performance. This in itself generates a sensation of power, in the knowledge of the weight of the train being hauled, coupled with a feeling of pride in the achievement. Coasting downgrade at maximum permitted speed, with only the track and wind noise audible, there was no impression of the size of the train, or the effort needed to move it uphill. The provision of train air brakes contributed to the ability to control speed precisely.

The power being developed on the climb to Church Stretton has already been mentioned. It offers an excellent testimony to the Class 37/7 concept of a 120-tonne prime mover. Even so, allowing 10 minutes for the various checks there was very little gain on net schedule of 87 minutes between Shrewsbury and Hereford. Net average speed of 36mph reflects both the heavy climbing and the 56mph romp from Craven Arms to Moreton-on-Lugg. The same applied for the final leg to Newport, with net schedule and net running time both being 74 minutes, representing an average of 35.2mph. With a relatively low horsepower per ton of 1.2 it was to be expected that considerable use would be made of full power. On this run No 37906 was driven flat out for 57% of the total running time. Such running was nothing special; it represented a normal duty. Yet the Class 37/9 performed in exemplary fashion in such circumstances and the above record shows what the type can do.

Chapter 8

Class 37 Personality Profiles

n any class of locomotives there will always be some which become better known than others. This is often the case with classes which spend much of their time on passenger work. Freight motive power is usually less in the public gaze and, unless subject to special distinction, is taken very much for granted, its world a largely closed book. In a class of 309, it is inevitable that some will become personalities. This chapter looks at three Class 37s which fall into this category and explains the background. Perhaps ironically, all three have put in more work on freight than passenger work.

D6700/37119/37350

t was on Christmas Eve 1960, that D6700 departed from Liverpool Street station for the first time. Delivered literally hours before performing its first passenger turn, the pioneer English Electric Type 3 diesel (later Class 37) could hardly have expected to be enjoying a new lease of life nearly 30 years later. Those years have seen a great change, not only to D6700, but to the whole railway environment in which the locomotive has performed so reliably. The first nine years were spent largely on the Great Eastern, being allocated to Stratford depot, in East London. Sterling work on passengers duties, albeit over fairly kind terrain, was followed by an increase in freight turns, as the Brush Type 4 locomotives (Class 47) took command of passenger trains.

An original livery of all-over dark green, with lion and wheel crest, was 'enlivened' by the eventual addition of a yellow warning panel, and later a full yellow nose end. Whilst at Doncaster Works in June 1969, 6700 (minus its D prefix) received standard blue livery and in February 1974 was renumbered 37119, taking up a position at the end of the numerical series covering the split headcode examples.

In January 1968 the locomotive went to the Research Department at Derby, prior to being loaned to Haymarket depot, Edinburgh the following month. On 29 February 1968, D6700 commenced push-pull trials between Edinburgh and Glasgow with five coaches, of which BSK E34500 had been fitted with driving controls. High speed runs, up to 90mph, began on 29 March, yet within a few weeks D6700 was back at Stratford.

Following the 1969 general overhaul, the loco was transferred to March (31B) in October 1969 and to Thornaby (51L) two years later. After renumbering, there were moves to Gateshead (March 1975), Tinsley (October 1975), Thornaby (February 1976), Healey Mills (September 1979), Thornaby (for a third time in November 1979), Stratford (July 1981), Immingham (October 1982), Gateshead (May 1983) and Immingham again (July 1985).

During the third spell at Thornaby, 37119 had twin fuel tanks fitted (October 1980) followed by a repaint, being observed resplendent in standard blue livery on 16 October 1980. Other previous modifications included the removal of the steam-heat boiler and the fitting in 1977 of dual brakes.

In March 1988, this venerable locomotive emerged from Crewe Works in its original green livery (though with full yellow nose ends) and renumbered 37350 following its fitting with CP7 bogies, thus beginning a new chapter in an already full life. In May 1988, 37350 moved back to original haunts at Stratford, before transfer to Cardiff in November. By April 1989, 37350 was one of 100 of the class allocated to Cardiff where it was a member of the South Wales Petroleum fleet (sub-Sector FPEK).

D6875/37175

t is surprising how some members of Class 37 retained their original allocations for so long. Indeed, it is only in recent years, with exchanges following refurbishment, that some examples have been transferred for the first time. From new in September 1963 until October 1982, D6875 was based at Cardiff. It would have participated in the various freight (primarily coal) and passenger turns covered by that depot and led an unremarkable life.

Top:
Barely a month old, D6700 stands on Stratford depot on 2 January 1961. *A. Swain*

Above:
Stratford again, this time 15 December 1968. D6700 has acquired its second livery style, with the addition of small yellow nose end warning panels. *D. L. Percival*

Top:
Converted to Class 37/3 and renumbered No 37350, the precursor of the type departs
Crewe with a Coedbach to Mossend working on 2 April 1988. *D. I. Rapson*

Above:
No 37350 sets off from Tyne Yard with a special for Carlisle on 5 April 1989. *N. E. Stead*

77

Above:
On 14 January 1980, when this picture was taken, No 37175 was a Cardiff machine. This accounts for its use on what the photographer assumes to be the 08.00 from Hereford, here at Paddington. *A. O. Wynn*

Below:
No 37175's reallocation to Eastfield from October 1982 was in connection with trials with CP5 bogies. By the time this undated photograph was taken the engine had received a black-painted blanking plate over its indicator box and a headlight. It is seen negotiating the Horseshoe Curve on the West Highland line. *P. J. Robinson*

Concern over running gear wear on the curving track of the West Highland led to the Railway Technical Centre staff designing a self-steering bogie. The concept was not new and previous research showed it could offer savings in tyre wear. The result was the production of what became known as the CP5 bogie. No 37175 emerged from Doncaster after an Intermediate overhaul on 15 July 1983 and went north. In the next three years it proved that the CP5 bogie suffered about 30% less running gear wear than standard Class 37 bogies.

When refurbished and ETS-equipped Class 37/4s arrived at Eastfield, No 37175, which had been allocated there from Cardiff, was displaced from its regular work. It was decided, therefore, to continue to take advantage of its self-steering abilities in an area where many of the lines were even more sharply curved than in Scotland – the china clay branches in Cornwall. Allocation to Laira from May 1986 brought the unprecedented sight of a Scottie dog running around the West Country with a locomotive attached! Displaced again, following the arrival of a batch of Class 37/5s, this time a new home was made at Inverness from October 1987. Its work off that depot has been on freight, primarily to the south. Indeed, since its last E exam at Eastfield on 7 May 1986, it had only run 3,340hr to the end of March 1989. Compared to the other two examples considered here, No 37175 was only averaging 1,160hr per annum, against 2,040 for No 37425 and 1,750 for No 37350.

During March 1989 it visited Springburn Works and exchanged its CP5 bogies for a conventional pair. Whilst the trial had proved to be an engineering success, conversion of a 30-year-old bogie on a large scale was not justified economically.

6992/37292/37425 *Concrete Bob*

6992 was one of a batch of 35 units which went new to Cardiff Canton depot. The depot already had a large complement of Class 37s to cover freight traffic in South Wales at a time when there was still a substantial coal traffic from the valleys. It was Vulcan Foundry No D981 and English Electric No 3552, and entry to service came on 5 July 1965.

In 1979-80 the decision was taken to examine the possibility of uprating the 12CSVT engine in a Class 37 to deliver 2,000bhp. There was nothing remarkable in this; it was, after all, the same power per cylinder as Class 50 diesels had produced from new in 1967 and DP2 since 1962. In opting for this rating in Class 37 some redesign work was deemed necessary by the BRB engineers. Whereas a standard Class 37 has just two stages of field weakening in its traction motors to deliver full engine output across a wide speed band, with Class 50 three stages are used. It was accordingly felt necessary to opt for three stages in No 37292 and a Class 50 style control was fitted. To ensure an adequate supply of fuel to the cylinders, Class 50 fuel pumps were exchanged with the previous standard Class 37 ones.

Reallocation to Eastfield came from May 1981, followed in October of that year by a further move to Motherwell. Here, deployment on the arduous Hunterston to Ravenscraig turns provided a stern test for the uprated power unit. The extra power it offered was appreciated by drivers, particularly in getting away from Hunterston. Things went well for the next three years; there were no particular problems, though the non-standard components associated with the uprating hit the locomotive's availability, as they were not to hand at Motherwell. Whilst the uprating was proved as practical, the business managers decided they did not want it. A classified repair came in the midst of the life-extension programme and No 37292 entered works in the late summer of 1985 for this treatment and fitting for ETS.

Renumbering to No 37425 came in January 1986 whilst still in Crewe; release came on April. Rated at the standard 1,750bhp, it went back to Eastfield, primarily for West Highland duties. Naming as *Concrete Bob*, to commemorate the civil engineer Sir Robert McAlpine (who was involved in the construction of the Mallaig extension), was on 14 October 1986. Arrival of Class 156 Super Sprinters on the route from January 1989 caused the locomotive to be displaced to Cardiff Canton, where it was able to help with the locomotive power problems caused by the temporary withdrawal of the Class 155s.

March it put in some time working stone traffic from Westbury to Banbury in the company of a Class 37/3 before moving to Tinsley towards the end of that month.

Above:
During its spell at Laira, No 37175 crosses Moorswater Viaduct with a short train of clayhoods in August 1986. *C. R. Holland*

Below:
During its spell on the Ravenscraig turns, No 37292 and No 37155 accelerate through Kilwinning with iron ore from Hunterston on 9 August 1982. *A. O. Wynn*

Bottom:
Renumbered to No 37425, the 'personality' locomotive makes a trial trip after undergoing a HGR at Crewe. Having arrived at Bangor as pilot to No 33002 on the 11.17 ex-Crewe, it will return on the 14.20 to Cardiff. Return to traffic came seven days later on 9 April 1985. *David N. Clough*

Appendix 1

Table of Particulars
By M. HUNT

Original Running No	EE Contract No	EE Rotation No	Vulcan Works No	RS&H No	Total delivered
6700-6741	CCL 1031	2863-2904	D579-620		42 (a)
6742-6768	CCM 1114	3034-3060	D696-722		27
6769-6778	CCM 1114	3061-3070		8315-8324	10 (b)
6779-6795	CCN 1239	3206-3222		8325-8342	17
6796-6818	CCP 1267	3225-3247	D750-772		23
6819-6828	CCP 1304	3264-3273		8379-8388	10
6829-6838	CCP 1304	3274-3283	D803-812		10
6839-6858	CCP 1304	3314-3333	D813-832		20
6859-6868	CCP 1304	3337-3346		8390-8399	10
6869-6878	CCP 1304	3347-3356	D833-842		10
6879-6898	CCP 1304	3357-3376		8400-8419	20
6899-6918	CCP 1304	3377-3396	D843-862		20
6919-6938	CCR 1320	3405-3424	D863-882		20
6939-6958	CCS 1362	3496-3515	D927-946		20
6959-6999 6600-6608	CCS 1362	3519-3568	D948-997		50

Notes: a = ordered January 1959   b = ordered February 1960
Not all construction numbers are in strict sequence with running numbers.

Appendix 2

Leading Dimensions
By M. HUNT

SUB-CLASS 37/0
Locomotives surviving in this sub-class remain essentially in the 'as-built' form. The entire Class 37 fleet, of course, once existed exclusively in this condition, and conveniently divided into two major groups as outlined in the text.

Phase I series
This series comprises the early locomotives, formerly numbered D6700-D6818, and later renumbered as 37.119, 37.001-37.118 respectively. The first order was placed in January 1959, and they included front end communicating doors and two-part route indicator boxes, together with warning horns located in the nose ends.
Leading dimensions and particulars:
Weight in running order: 108 tons (nominal)

TE Max: 55,500lb at 24.1% adhesion (Phase I locomotives) at 23.6% adhesion (Phase II locomotives), with 2,600A total generator current
TE continuous: 35,000lb at 13.6mph, with 1,800A total generator current
Rail hp continuous: 1,250hp (932kW)
Full engine output: Available between 10 and 79mph
Total wheelbase: 50ft 8in
Bogie centres: 37ft 2in
Bogie wheelbase: 13ft 6in
Wheel diameter: 3ft 7in new; 3ft 4½in (min permissible)
Clearance to rail level: 7½in (new wheels); 6in (max permissible wheel wear)
Weight of bogie: 19.4 tons in running order
Width: 8ft 8⅝in over body; 8ft 11⅝in over handrails
Length: 61ft 6in over buffers
Height: 12ft 10½in overall
Min radius curve negotiable: 4 chains
Max speed: 90mph*
Route availability: 5
Multiple-unit working: Blue Star
Max axle loading: 18 tons nominal (Phase I locomotives); 17.55 tons max (Phase II locomotives)

Fuel tanks: Engine fuel 800gal (3,636.8 litres)
Boiler fuel (in one tank) 120gal (545.5 litres), plus 30gal emergency tank
Total: 950gal
Lubricating oil: 120gal (545.5 litres)
Cooling water capacity: 160gal (727.4 litres)
Boiler water tank (water column filling only) 800gal (3,636.8 litres)
Sand boxes 8cu ft (compressed air operated)
Brakes: Compressed air and hand brakes on locomotive, and, originally vacuum brake equipment for train giving proportional braking on the locomotive. The class was later converted for dual air/vacuum train braking. Brake force is 82.5% (Phase I) and 80.7% (Phase II) of locomotive weight in working order.

*Since the introduction of modified Class 37 locomotives with a lower gear ratio, this has been changed to an 80mph operational 'ceiling', thus eliminating any risk of traction motor overspeeding when operating Class 37 units of differing gear ratios in multiple.

POWER EQUIPMENT
12-cylinder, four-stroke 'vee'-form oil engine; charge-cooled and turbo-supercharged; English Electric Co Type 12 CSVT (Mark II), rated continuously at 1,750bhp (1,305kW) at 850rpm. Engine speed variable between 450 and 850rpm.
Idling speed: 470rpm no load; 450rpm on power
Max power: 525hp developed at idling speed
Direction of crankshaft rotation looking on 'free' end – anti-clockwise:
Cylinder bore 10in (254.0mm)
Piston stroke 12in (304.8mm)
Compression ratio 11.7:1
Firing order: 1 5 3 6 2 4 'B' bank**
          6 2 4 1 5 3 'A' bank
**'B' bank is the 'battery isolating switch side' of the engine, and carries the governor; No 1 cylinders are furthest from the flywheel.
Fuel injector: CAV type BKB 200T 5087b nozzle holder; CAV type BDL 160T 6332 nozzle (6 hole)
Blow-off pressure of nozzle: 3,000lb/sq in
Fuel injection pump type: CAV BPF 1CC 200BS 6436

Turbo-supercharger: Napier HP 200Z INT or HP210, two in number, blowing speed 13,500rpm at full load

Traction generator: English Electric Co 10-pole Type EE 822/10G, weighing 13,500lb. Self-ventilated at 6,500cu ft/min at 850rpm. Continuous rating, full field – 1,107kW, 1,800A, 615V at 850rpm.

Auxiliary generator: English Electric Co 8-pole Type EE 911/5C. Self-ventilated. Weight 1,870lb. Continuous rating, full field – 66kW, 600A, 110V at 450/850rpm.

Traction motors: 6×English Electric Co 4-pole Type EE 538/A. Weight (with pinion) 4,987lb. Nose-suspended, axle-hung, force-ventilated at 2,500cu ft/min. Continuous rating, full field – 600A 300V. Ratio of single reduction spur gears: 53:18 (2.944:1).

AUXILIARY EQUIPMENT:

Traction motor blowers: 2×Keith Blackman, special 22½in AR (W) fans.

Traction motor blower motors: 2×English Electric Co Type EE 750/26G, 2-pole continuous rating, full field – 14.4hp, 110V, 124A at 2,480-2,500rpm.

Radiator fan: 60in diameter; engine driven through gearbox

Air compressor: Worthington-Simpson type MSV38S

Air compressor motor: English Electric Co Type EE 758/A. Continuous rating – 6.1hp, 110V, 60A at 1,450rpm.

Vacuum exhausters: 2×Northey, lightweight, Type 125 RE

Vacuum exhauster motors: 2×English Electric Co Type EE 762/2B four pole. Continuous rating – Maintaining (full field) 4.25hp, 110V, 37A at 1,250rpm. Release (32.6% field) 6.5hp, 110V, 58A at 1,850rpm.

Fuel supply pump motor: English Electric Co Type TFZ 97915, 2-pole. Totally enclosed. Continuous rating, full field – ⅛hp, 110V, 1.56A at 1,420rpm.

Fuel supply pump: Varley DH2 or DH25.

Lubricating oil priming pump motor: English Electric Co Type TFZ 97924. Totally enclosed. 2-pole. ½hr rating, full field 1.25hp, 110V, 11.0A at 1,900rpm.

Storage battery: DP Battery Co Type RSKB158, M/3 cells, 48 in number. 158AH capacity at the 5hr rate.

Carriage warming steam generator: Clayton Type RO-2500/3, 2,000lb/hour or RO-2500 Mk I or Mk II 2,500lb of steam per hour.

PHASE II SERIES

This series comprises later locomotives, formerly numbered D6819-D6999, and D6600-D6608. Later renumbered 37.283, 37.120-37.299 and 37.300-37.308 respectively. The front-end communicating doors were omitted, permitting a central route indicator display panel. Warning horns were repositioned on the cab roof, and this elevates the overall height to 13ft 0¾in. Locomotive weight in running order is 104.6 tons. Sand box capacity is 6cu ft. There are detail changes to the CAV fuel injection equipment viz:

Injectors: Injection pumps: Type BPF 1CC 200CS 6570
Nozzle holder: Type BKB 200T 5131b
Nozzle: Type BDL 140T 6332

Several variations on the basic EE 822 traction generator are installed, principally the EE 822/10G, 13G and 16J. This reflects improvements over the years spanned by construction. There are also changes to some auxiliaries. The air compressor is now a Westinghouse Brake & Signal Co Type 2EC38B, and the vacuum exhausters are Reavell Type FRU 5¼in×10in, driven by English Electric Type EE 762/4C 4-pole motors, rated at (continuous, full field) 2.75hp, 25A, 110V at 715rpm (maintaining), and, for release, at 5.75hp, 33A at 1,430rpm.

The final 50 locomotives (D6959-D6999, D6600-D6608) incorporated significant updating of control gear. These locomotives incorporated voltage balance rather than current balance wheelslip detection equipment, and the power circuit featured negative-to-ground earthing and associated control circuitry, such as that for power control, and could be conveniently referred to as 'Phase III'.

Dual braking throughout the class necessitated the installation of a second air compressor. The first 10 locomotives that were fitted with dual brakes were equipped with Westinghouse 3VC75 compressors. These have been replaced by 3VC50 machines, which have also been used on all subsequent conversions. Both compressors are sited in No 1 nose end compartment.

SUB-CLASS 37/3

Nos 37.350-37.381. These are original or unrefurbished locomotives which have had their bogies replaced by modified ones incorporating new axles and detail changes to the transoms and traction motors, including a lower traction motor reduction gear ratio. These modified bogies, designated CP7, are also those used in the Class 37 life-extension programme (see next section of summary). The modified EE 538/A traction motors have been recoded EE 538/5A by British Rail, ie the type code coincides with that of the motors deployed on Class 50. The reduction ratio has been changed to 59:16 (3.6875:1). In consequence, the maximum tractive effort is 56,180lb whilst the continuous rating is now 41,250lb at 11.4mph. Maximum speed is restricted to 80mph as a result of the change in gear ratio, with the full power speed range 7-68mph.

Summary of Class 37 life-extension programme

This has been referred to in the text, and has involved complete refurbishment, plus the removal of the original and ageing dc generator group and replacement by alternators, together with their associated rectifiers. Bogies of the CP7 type have replaced those originally installed. There are numerous detail changes. Fuel capacity has been increased by converting the redundant boiler water tanks to provide 1,690gal (7,682.9 litres) of capacity.

SUB-CLASS 37/4

Nos 37.401-37.431. Refurbished locomotives converted out of the final batch of 50 original units and fitted for electric train supply (ETS). The traction alternator is a Brush Electrical Machines Type BA 1005A, which is a 12-pole three-phase, star-connected brushless machine. There is also a dual-wound auxiliary/ETS three-phase brushless alternator set of Type BAH 701A. This has two regulated, rectified outputs, one at 110V dc to supply the existing auxiliary system, and one at 850V dc supplying up to 150kW for the train supply (ETH Index 38). The traction motor reduction ratio, as with all refurbished locomotives, is 59:16, and the tractive effort details are as follows:

Max tractive effort: 57,440lb
Tractive effort at continuous rating: 41,250lb at 11.4mph
Power at rail: 1,254hp (935kW)
Full power speed range: 7-68mph
Route availability: 5
Weight: 108 tonnes

DETAILS OF ALTERNATOR SET:
BA 1005A (traction)/BAE 508A (exciter). Continuous ratings through rectifier, with engine set at 1,750hp:
No train supply: 1,149kW, 860V dc, 1,336A dc @ 850rpm.
                     1,148kW, 638V dc, 1,800A dc @ 850rpm

Full train supply: 993kW, 903V dc, 1,100A dc @ 850rpm.
                       990kW, 550V dc, 1,800A dc @ 850rpm
Train supply/auxiliary machine: BAH 701A (8-pole)/BAE 508B (exciter).
ETS winding: 150kW, 850V dc, 176A dc, 450/850rpm
Auxiliary winding: 70kW, 110V dc, 636A dc, 450/850 rpm

SUB-CLASS 37/5

This is a freight version of Class 37/4. In place of the dual-wound auxiliary/ETS alternator, a Brush Type BAA 606A 8-pole 70kW three-phase star-connected brushless auxiliary alternator is deployed, with only one (110V) dc rectified output. For other details, see Class 37/4. The locomotive weight is 105 tonnes. Some units have slow speed equipment.

Max tractive effort: 55,590lb (Series 1 conversions)
56,720lb (Series 2 conversions)

Continuous tractive effort is identical to sub-Class 37/4

SUB-CLASS 37/7

This is a further freight variant, but ballasted to provide for greater adhesion. The adhesive weight has been increased to 120 tonnes, and route availability is 7. Locomotives 37.796-37.803 have a GEC alternator group in accordance with BR's policy for dual-sourcing of equipment. The traction alternator is the GEC Type G564 AZ 10-pole 1,200kW brushless machine, whose rectified output is continuously rated between 620V, 1,800A, and 880V, 1,280A, both at 850rpm. The auxiliary alternator is the GEC Type G659 AZ, whose continuous rating (rectified output) is 110V, 636A over the range 425/900rpm. The exciters are of Types G658 AZ, G658 BY respectively. All other locomotives have Brush equipment, described under Class 37/5, whose ratings are virtually identical, to suit the existing traction motors, etc.

Max tractive effort: 62,680lb (Brush)
62,580lb (GEC)

For other details, see Class 37/4.

SUB-CLASS 37/9

These are basically re-engined locomotives of Class 37/7 type, and all have slow speed control. They are acting as mobile test-beds for the evaluation of manufacturers' prototype engines for traction service. Nos 37.901-37.904 employ a Mirrlees-Blackstone Type 6MB275T six-cyliner in-line oil engine rated at 1,800hp (1,342.3kW) at 1,000rpm, married to the same Brush alternator group as described under Class 37/5. Some engine details are:

Cylinder bore: 275mm
Piston stroke: 305mm
Engine governor: Woodward PG type
Turbocharger: Brown Boveri Type VTC 254
Max tractive effort: 63,760lb

Locomotives 37.905 and 37.906 have a Ruston Type 6RK270T engine installed, which also has six cylinders in-line, and delivers the same output as Nos 37.901-4, but at 900rpm. This engine has been developed directly from the original English Electric RK series, but has an increased cylinder bore. Some engine details are:

Cylinder bore: 270mm
Piston stroke: 305mm
Bryce Type FCVAB individual fuel injection pumps, and Bryce fuel injectors.
Engine governor: Regulateurs Europa Type 1131A/4G
Turbocharger: Brown-Boveri Type VTC 254
Max tractive effort: 63,520lb

The same GEC alternator group is employed as found on Nos 37.796-803.

Appendix 3

Naming Details of Class 37 Locomotives

No	Name	Where Named	When
37012	*Loch Rannoch* (removed 6/86)	Fort William	31 March 1982
37026	*Loch Awe* (removed 7/86)	Glasgow Queen St	6 October 1981
37027	*Loch Eil* (removed 2/87)	Glasgow Queen St	6 October 1981
37043	*Loch Lomond* (removed 6/86)	Glasgow Queen St	6 October 1981
37059	*Port of Tilbury*	Tilbury Riverside	26 September 1988
37062	*British Steel Corby* (removed 2/87)	BSC Lackenby	30 September 1985
37066	*British Steel Workington* (removed 4/87)	BSC Lackenby	30 September 1985
37068	*Grainflow* (a)	Ely	23 September 1987
37069	*Thornaby TMD*	Thornaby	29 September 1986
37071	*British Steel Skinningrove* (removed 3/87)	BSC Lackenby	30 September 1985
37077	*British Steel Shelton* (removed 7/87)	BSC Lackenby	30 September 1985
37078	*Teesside Steelmaster* (removed 2/87)	BSC Lackenby	4 July 1984
37081	*Loch Long* (removed 5/86)	Glasgow Queen St	6 October 1981
37095	*British Steel Teesside* (removed 3/87)	BSC Lackenby	30 September 1985
37111	*Loch Eil Outward Bound* (removed 7/86)	Loch Eil	20 April 1985
37113	*Radio Highland*	BRML Doncaster	1 September 1989
37114	*Dunrobin Castle*	Dunrobin	30 June 1985
37180	*Sir Dyfed/County of Dyfed* (removed 3/87)	Carmarthen	28 May 1981
37188	*Jimmy Shand* (removed 5/89)	Oban	10 May 1985
37191	*International Youth Year 1985* (removed 11/85)	Glasgow	21 January 1985
37196	*Tre Pol and Pen* (removed 5/87)	Truro	16 July 1985
37207	*William Cookworthy* (removed 7/87)	St Austell	27 May 1982
37229	*The Cardiff Rod Mill* (removed 10/88)	Cardiff	May 1984
37235	*Coal Merchants' Assocation of Scotland*	Aberdeen	3 November 1987
37260	*Radio Highland* (removed 8/89)	Dingwall	7 July 1984
37261	*Caithness*	Wick	14 June 1985
37262	*Dounreay*	Thurso	14 June 1985
37275	*Stainless Pioneer*	Tinsley	16 December 1988
37310	*British Steel Ravenscraig* (b)	Motherwell	4 March 1986
37311	*British Steel Hunterston* (b)	Motherwell	4 March 1986
37312	*Clyde Iron* (b)	Motherwell	24 July 1986
37314	*Dalzell* (b)	Motherwell	25 July 1986
37320	*Shap Fell* (c)	Motherwell	23 July 1986
37321	*Gartcosh* (c)	Motherwell	23 July 1986
37322	*Imperial* (c)	Motherwell	24 July 1986
37323	*Clydesdale* (c)	Motherwell	23 July 1986
37324	*Clydebridge* (c)	Motherwell	27 July 1986
37325	*Lanarkshire Steel* (c)	Motherwell	6 August 1986
37326	*Glengarnock* (c)	Motherwell	23 July 1986
37358	*P&O Containers*	Southampton	13 April 1988
37401	*Mary Queen of Scots*	Linlithgow	4 November 1985
37402	*Oor Wullie*	Glasgow Central	14 December 1985
37403	*Isle of Mull* (removed 11/88)	Oban	3 January 1986
37403	*Glendarroch*	Eastfield	November 1988
37404	*Ben Cruachan*	Oban	3 January 1986
37405	*Strathclyde Region*	Glasgow Queen St	11 April 1986
37406	*The Saltire Society*	Eastfield	27 June 1986
37407	*Loch Long*	Eastfield	August 1986
37408	*Loch Rannoch*	Eastfield	1 September 1986
37409	*Loch Awe*	Eastfield	27 August 1986
37410	*Aluminium 100*	Lynemouth	21 September 1986

37411	*The Institution of Railway Signal Engineers*	Ft William	28 May 1987
37412	*Loch Lomond* (removed 5/89)	Eastfield	10 March 1987
37413	*Loch Eil Outward Bound*	Eastfield	March 1987
37417	*Highland Region*	Inverness	16 December 1985
37418	*An Comunn Gaidhealach*	Edinburgh Waverley	10 October 1986
37420	*The Scottish Hosteller*	Inverness	28 June 1986
37423	*Sir Murray Morrison 1873-1948*	Fort William	18 May 1988
37424	*Glendarroch* (removed 10/88)	Glasgow Queen St	9 December 1987
37425	*Sir Robert McAlpine/Concrete Bob*	Ft William/Glenfinnan	14 October 1986
37426	*Y Lein Fach/Vale of Rheidol*	Aberystwyth	5 May 1986
37427	*Bont Y Bermo*	Barmouth	13 April 1986
37428	*David Lloyd George*	Pwllheli	16 May 1987
37429	*Sir Dyfed/County of Dyfed* (removed 7/87)	Cardiff Canton	2 April 1987
37429	*Eisteddfod Genedlaethol*	Porthmadog	4 August 1987
37430	*Cwmbran*	Cwmbran	11 May 1986
37431	*Sir Powys/County of Powys*	Llandrindod Wells	17 June 1987
37501	*Teesside Steelmaster*	Thornaby	21 February 1987
37502	*British Steel Teesside*	Thornaby	March 1987
37503	*British Steel Shelton*	Thornaby	24 July 1987
37504	*British Steel Corby*	Thornaby	March 1987
37505	*British Steel Workington*	Thornaby	April 1987
37506	*British Steel Skinningrove*	Thornaby	March 1987
37507	*Hartlepool Pipe Mill*	Hartlepool	4 December 1987
37511	*Stockton Haulage*	Middlesbrough	24 February 1988
37512	*Thornaby Demon*	Thornaby	13 May 1987
37667	*Wensleydale*	Thornaby	September 1988
37668	*Leyburn*	Thornaby	September 1988
37671	*Tre Pol and Pen*	Laira	22 July 1987
37672	*Freight Transport Association*	Stratford-upon-Avon	14 September 1987
37675	*William Cookworthy*	Laira	August 1987
37688	*Great Rocks*	Hindlow	23 June 1988
37698	*Coedbach*	Coed Bach	21 September 1988
37702	*Taff Merthyr*	Cardiff Canton	20 November 1989
37711	*Tremorfa Steelworks*	Cardiff Tidal Sdgs	9 November 1988
37712	*The Cardiff Rod Mill*	Cardiff Tidal Sdgs	9 November 1988
37799	*Sir Dyfed/County of Dyfed* (d)	Cardiff Canton	7 November 1987
37800	*Glo Cymru*	Aberthaw	27 September 1986
37801	*Aberthaw/Aberddawan*	Aberthaw	27 September 1986
37888	*Petrolea*	Stratford	27 May 1988
37892	*Ripple Lane*	Ripple Lane	17 October 1987
37901	*Mirrlees Pioneer*	Cardiff Canton	3 December 1986
37905	*Vulcan Enterprise*	Cardiff Canton	3 February 1987

Notes

a) 37068 carried the number 37356 between June 1988 and June 1989.

b) 37310-2/4 have since regained their former identities (37152, 37156, 37137 and 37190 respectively).

c) 37320-6 have similarly regained their former identities (37026, 37037, 37049, 37088, 37099, 37108 and 37111 respectively). 37026 and 37111 have thus carried two names.

d) 37799 is the third member of the class to carry the *Sir Dyfed/County of Dyfed* nameplates (37180 and 37429 being the others).

Allocation History

Allocation data is correct to 19 September 1990.

Note: re – date renumbered; in – date re-instated following withdrawal.

1958 No.	TOPS No.	TOPS ren	Ent. Serv	1st Dep	Shed	Date Trans	Shed	Date Trans	Shed	Date Trans	Shed	Date Trans	Shed	Date Trans	Shed	Date Trans
D6600	37300	37429	08.65	86A	87A	10.71	re	11.73	ED	02.85	7ML	07.85	CF	01.86	re	03.86
D6601	37301	37412	09.65	87E	86A	09.67	87A	10.71	re	05.74	ED	03.85				
					re	10.85	IS	01.89	LA	02.89						
D6602	37302	37416	09.65	87E	86A	09.67	87A	10.71	re	03.74	7ED	03.85	re	10.85	IS	01.86
					TI	10.87										
D6603	37303	37271	09.65	87E	86A	12.66	82A	05.67	87E	08.67	86A	12.68				
					86A	10.69	87A	10.71	re	02.74	CF	02.86	TI	10.87	re	01.89
D6604	37304	37272	10.65	86A	82A	05.67	87E	09.67	86A	10.69	87A	10.71				
					re	03.74	ED	01.85	CF	02.86	TI	10.87	re	01.89		
D6605	37305	37407	10.65	87E	86A	12.66	82A	05.67	87E	09.67	86A	10.69				
					87A	10.71	ED	01.85	re	08.85	CF	01.89	IM	11.89	ED	04.90
D6606	37306	37273	10.65	86A	82A	05.67	87E	09.67	86A	10.69						
					87A	10.71	re	03.74	7LE	05.731	CF	02.86	re	02.89		
D6607	37307	37403	11.65	87E	86A	12.66	82A	05.67	87E	10.67	86A	10.69				
					87A	10.71	re	08.85	CF	02.86						
D6608	37308	37274	11.65	87E	86A	12.66	82A	05.67	87E	10.67	86A	10.69				
					87A	10.71	re	03.74	ML	07.85	CF	01.86	re	02.89		
D6700	37119	37350	12.60	30A	DRC	01.68	30A	04.68	31B	10.69	51L	10.71	re	01.74		
					GD	03.75	TI	10.75	TE	02.76	HM	09.79	TE	11.79	SF	07.81
					IM	10.82	GD	05.83	IM	07.85	re	03.88	SF	05.88	CF	11.88
D6701	37001	37707	12.60	30A	41C	07.67	41A	11.67	51L	05.70	re	03.74	TI	07.81		
					SF	01.82	re	12.87	IM	09.89	ED	11.89				
D6702	37002	37351	12.60	30A	32A	05.61	30A	07.61	41C	09.67	41A	11.67	51L	05.70		
					re	01.74	HM	10.81	TE	01.82	IM	02.82	re	05.89		
D6703	37003		12.60	30A	31B	05.61	30A	07.61	41C	09.67	41A	11.67	51L	05.70	re	01.74
					GD	09.79	TE	01.82	HM	02.82	TE	05.82	GD	10.82	TI	07.87
					IM	01.90										
D6704	37004		01.61	30A	32B	05.61	30A	07.61	41C	10.67	41A	11.67	51L	05.70	re	03.74
					ED	01.81	SF	03.81	GD	09.84	ED	09.86	ML	10.87	SF	11.87
					TE	05.89										
D6705	37005	37501	01.61	30A	31B	02.61	30A	07.61	41C	11.67	41A	05.68				
					51L	05.70	re	01.74	GD	09.79	TE	01.82	GD	01.83	CF	07.85
					re	04.86	TE	01.87								
D6706	37006	37798	01.61	31B	32A	02.61	30A	07.61	41C	11.67	41A	05.68				
					51L	05.70	re	03.74	HM	10.81	GD	09.84	CF	04.86	re	04.86
D6707	37007	37506	02.61	31B	30A	07.61	41C	12.67	41A	05.68	51L	05.70				
					re	02.74	GD	05.83	IM	07.85	CF	10.85	re	04.86	TE	01.87
D6708	37008	37352 / 37008	02.61	31B	30A	07.61	41C	10.67	41A	11.67	55C	07.70				
					52A	10.72	TE	09.73	re	03.74	GD	05.83	ED	09.86	TI	05.87
					re	06.88	re	07.89								
D6709	37009		02.61	30A	41C	12.67	41A	05.68	55C	07.70	51L	04.72	52A	11.72		
					TE	09.73	re	03.74	GD	05.83	TI	07.87				
D6710	37010		02.61	30A	56B	02.68	41A	10.68	55C	07.70	51L	04.72	52A	11.72		
					re	01.74	TE	05.74	HM	01.83	GD	09.84	TI	11.86	SF	09.87
					ML	10.88										
D6711	37011		03.61	30A	51L	10.68	52A	03.69	55C	01.70	31B	08.72	re	01.74		
					ED	06.81	IS	05.82	ED	10.82	SU	02.87	ED	05.87	WDN	08.87
D6712	37012		03.61	30A	51L	10.68	52A	03.69	51L	01.70	52A	03.70	30A	10.70		
					re	02.74										
					MR	05.74	SF	01.78	ED	01.81	ML	10.87	SF	11.87	TI	07.89
					CF	01.90										
D6713	37013		03.61	30A	41A	05.68	55C	07.70	31B	10.72	TE	02.74	re	02.74		
					GD	09.79	ED	08.80	HM	06.81	TI	05.82	GD	01.83	TI	05.83
					ED	05.84	TE	11.84	TI	01.87						
D6714	37014	37709	03.61	30A	41A	05.68	55C	07.70	31B	08.72	re	02.74				
					SF	02.78	ED	01.81	IS	10.81	ML	10.87	SF	10.87	re	02.88
					IM	04.90										
D6715	37015		05.61	30A	41A	05.68	55C	07.70	52A	10.72	MR	09.73	re	12.73		
					TE	02.74	GD	05.83	TI	05.87						
D6716	37016	37706	06.61	30A	41A	05.68	55C	07.70	D16	01.72	52A	10.72				
					MR	09.73	TE	02.74	re	03.74	ED	01.81	SF	02.81	HM	03.81
					SF	01.82	re	11.87	IM	04.90						
D6717	37017	37503	05.61	30A	41A	05.68	55C	07.70	D16	01.72	55C	01.72				
					31B	08.72	re	02.74	HM	05.81	ED	09.81	IS	05.82	ED	01.83
					IS	10.83	ED	10.84	CF	08.85	re	03.86	TE	01.87		
D6718	37018	37517	06.61	30A	41A	05.68	IM	09.73	re	01.74	HM	01.81				
					ED	01.81	SF	05.85	IM	08.85	IS	05.86	TE	01.87	re	04.87
D6719	37019		06.61	30A	41A	05.68	re	05.74	IM	10.74	SF	10.76	TE	02.78	TI	07.81
					SF	01.82	ML	07.87	SF	11.87	TI	07.89				

1958 No.	TOPS No.	TOPS ren	Ent. Serv	1st Dep	Shed Date Trans	Shed Date Trans	Shed Date Trans	Shed Date Trans	Shed Date Trans	Shed Date Trans
D6720	**37020**	**37702**	06.61	30A	41A 05.68	31B 08.68	30A 01.69	31B 10.69	41A 04.72	
					IM 09.73	re 02.74	SF 10.76	IM 10.76	TI 05.78	TE 01.79
					GD 05.83	ED 06.85	IM 07.85	CF 07.86	re 12.86	
D6721	**37021**	**37715**	07.61	32A	30A 09.61	31B 10.69	51L 10.71	re 02.74		
					IM 03.74	MR 01.76	SF 05.78	ED 01.81	SF 11.81	IS 05.85
					ED 01.86	ML 05.88	CF 07.88	re 11.88		
D6722	**37022**	**37512**	07.61	32A	32B 07.61	30A 09.61	31B 05.68	30A 01.69		
					31B 10.69	re 01.74	SF 05.78	ED 01.81	TE 08.86	re 01.87
D6723	**37023**		07.61	31B	30A 09.61	31B 05.68	re 02.74	SF 05.81	MR 05.82	
					HM 10.82	TE 12.82	TI 05.84	ML 05.87	ED 06.88	TE 05.89
D6724	**37024**	**37714**	08.61	31B	30A 09.61	31B 08.66	32B 01.67	31B 05.67	30A 02.68	
					31B 05.68	TE 02.74	re 02.74	IM 05.77	MR 09.79	TE 01.80
					MR 01.81	CF 04.81	TI 05.83	ML 05.87	ED 08.87	CF 05.88
					re 10.88					
D6725	**37025**		08.61	30A	TE 02.74	re 02.74	MR 02.77	SF 05.81	ED 06.81	IS 05.82
					ED 01.86	ML 10.87	ED 04.90	ED 08.90		
D6726	**37026**	**37320** **37026**	09.61	30A	re 02.74	SF 05.77	MR 10.77	ML 01.79		
					ED 02.80	ML 04.86	re 07.86	IM 05.88	ML 06.88	re 09.89
D6727	**37027**	**37519**	09.61	30A	re 03.74	SF 05.77	MR 10.77	ED 04.80	TE 03.87	
					re 08.87					
D6728	**37028**	**37505**	09.61	30A	41A 05.65	31B 04.66	re 02.74	GD 02.75	HM 02.78	
					ED 02.79	TE 09.85	CF 09.85	re 02.86	TE 01.87	
D6729	**37029**		10.61	30A	41A 05.65	31B 10.72	55C 03.73	re 11.73	MR 05.74	
					GD 08.78	TI 09.85	TE 03.86	TI 01.87		
D6730	**37030**	**37701**	10.61	50B	55C 10.69	31B 10.72	55C 10.72	GD 09.73	re 02.74	
					HM 10.82	TI 09.84	ML 08.85	ED 04.86	CF 07.86	re 12.86
D6731	**37031**		10.61	50B	55C 10.69	51L 01.70	52A 08.72	51L 10.72	GD 09.73	
					re 03.74	HM 03.75	GD 05.80	HM 10.82	TI 09.84	
D6732	**37032**	**37353** **37032**	03.62	50B	55C 10.69	41A 10.70	51L 05.71	52A 11.72		
					re 02.74	TE 03.74	GD 10.77	TE 01.81	TI 09.85	TE 03.86
					TI 01.87	re 06.88	re 06.89			
D6733	**37033**	**37719**	03.62	50B	55C 10.69	30A 01.72	re 10.73	MR 05.74	ED 01.81	
					IS 02.87	ML 05.88	CF 07.88	re 03.89		
D6734	**37034**	**37704**	03.62	50B	55C 10.69	31B 10.72	SF 09.73	re 02.74	MR 05.75	
					SF 05.81	ML 08.85	ED 12.85	CF 08.86	re 01.87	
D6735	**37035**		04.62	50B	55C 10.69	30A 08.72	31B 10.72	re 02.74	GD 03.74	
					MR 02.75	HM 05.31	IS 05.82	ED 01.86	IM 07.90	
D6736	**37036**	**37507**	04.62	50B	55C 10.69	41A 12.72	re 03.74	TE 07.74	MR 03.77	
					TE 07.83	TI 05.84	SF 08.85	CF 12.85	re 04.86	TE 01.87
D6737	**37037**	**37321** **37037**	05.62	50B	40B 08.72	41A 10.72	IM 09.73	re 01.74	SF 02.81	ED 03.81
					ML 12.85	re 07.86	ML 05.87	re 04.89		
D6738	**37038**		05.62	50B	55C 10.69	30A 08.72	31B 10.72	re 02.74	TI 03.74	
					SF 02.81	ED 03.81	ML 12.85	SF 05.88	ML 05.87	
					SF 05.88	CF 07.89	ML ??.??	TI ??.??		
D6739	**37039**	**37504**	05.62	50B	55C 10.69	41A 10.71	31B 10.72	re 02.74	SF 02.81	
					ED 02.81	re 03.86	CF 09.85	TI 01.87		
D6740	**37040**		06.62	50B	55C 10.69	re 02.74	TI 09.84	ML 05.87		
D6741	**37041**	**37520**	06.62	50B	51L 10.69	52A 10.70	31B 05.71	52A 04.72		
					TE 05.73	MR 03.74	re 03.74	SF 05.81	TI 05.84	ML 08.85
					ED 12.85	GD 03.86	SF 11.86	TE 09.87		
D6742	**37042**		06.62	41A	88A 09.62	41A 04.63	41A 04.64	52A 10.70	re 01.74	
					SF 09.73	HM 01.76	TE 10.76	TI 05.78	MR 09.78	TE 02.79
					IM 05.86	TE 05.89				
D6743	**37043**	**37354**	06.62	41A	88A 10.62	41A 04.63	41A 04.64	SF 09.73		
					re 02.74	MR 05.75	ED 04.80	TE 10.87	re 06.88	CF 02.89
					SF 07.89					
D6744	**37044**	**37710**	06.62	41A	41A 04.64	SF 09.73	re 02.74	ED 07.87	ML 10.87	
					Su 02.88	ML 02.88	CF 03.88	re 07.88		
D6745	**37045**	**37355** **37045**	07.62	41A	41A 04.64	52A 10.70	re 03.74	HM 01.76	TE 10.76	
					TI 09.86	re 06.88	re 05.90			
D6746	**37046**		07.62	41A	41A 04.64	41C 08.66	re 02.74			
					TE 02.78	ED 02.79	HM 06.81	TI 05.82	ED 07.87	TE 10.88
					ML 04.89	TE 05.89				
D6747	**37047**		07.62	41A	41C 04.66	31B 08.67	30A 02.71	re 03.74	MR 05.74	
					SF 05.81	TI 05.84	SF 09.87	TI 07.89		
D6748	**37048**		08.62	41A	41A 04.64	30A 06.67	55C 10.69	52A 01.70	IM 03.74	
					re 03.74	GD 08.74	TE 02.78	MR 01.81	TI 05.83	SF 09.87
					IM 10.88	TE 05.89				
D6749	**37049**	**37322** **37049**	08.62	41A	41A 04.64	32B 08.67	30A 01.68	55C 10.69		
					30A 07.71	re 12.73	MR 02.81	SF 05.81	ED 05.85	ML 11.85
					re 07.86	re 06.88				
D6750	**37050**	**37717**	08.62	41A	41A 04.64	D16 11.66	32B 08.67	31B 05.68		
					re 11.73	SF 05.81	SF 06.81	ED 07.81	SF 11.81	IS 06.86
					IM 05.88	CF 07.88	re 02.89			
D6751	**37051**		09.62	41A	41A 04.64	32B 08.67	re 02.74	ED 03.81	ML 05.87	
D6752	**37052**	**37713**	09.62	41A	41A 04.64	32B 08.67	31B 05.68	re 02.74	TE 05.86	
					MR 05.83	SF 09.85	CF 05.88	re 08.88		
D6753	**37053**		09.62	41A	41A 04.64	32B 08.67	30A 12.67	31B 03.69	re 02.74	
					GD 03.74	TE 02.78	SF 01.81	SF 09.85	TI 07.89	
D6754	**37054**		09.62	41A	41A 04.64	32B 08.67	31B 05.68	re 02.74	GD 03.74	
					MR 02.75	IM 10.88	TE 05.89			

1958 No.	TOPS No.	TOPS ren	Ent. Serv	1st Dep	Shed	Date Trans	Shed	Dat Trans	Shed	Date Trans	Shed	Date Trans	Shed	Date Trans	Shed	Date Trans
D6755	37055		09.62	51L	52A	06.64	51L	09.64	30A	02.72	51L	04.72	re	02.74		
					IM	05.74	MR	05.75	TE	02.76	MR	06.77	GD	10.77	IM	01.78
					MR	09.79	TE	01.80	SF	01.81	TI	07.89				
D6756	37056		09.62	51L	52A	06.64	51L	09.64	52A	03.70	31B	05.71	re	02.74		
					TE	02.76	MR	06.77	GD	10.77	TI	05.78	ML	01.79	ED	12.85
					ML	01.86	IS	05.86	TE	09.86	re	01.87				
D6757	37057		10.62	51L	52A	01.70	TE	05.73	52A	01.70	re	02.74	IM	02.75		
					MR	06.75	GD	05.76	SF	10.76	TE	02.78	SF	01.81	TI	07.89
					ML	09.90										
D6758	37058		10.62	51L	51L	12.67	re	03.74	TE	01.82	GD	10.82	TI	10.87	TE	10.89
D6759	37059		10.62	51L	52A	01.70	30A	10.71	31B	10.72	51L	03.73	re	11.73		
					IM	02.75	MR	05.75	GD	05.76	GD	01.87	TI	10.87		
D6760	37060	37705	10.62	51L	52A	01.70	51L	08.72	re	03.74	IM	03.75	SF	10.76		
					ED	01.81	SF	02.81	ML	08.85	SF	10.85	re	10.87	IM	04.90
D6761	37061	37799	10.62	51L	52A	01.70	re	02.74	TE	01.82	GD	10.82	TE	02.86		
					CF	03.86	re	08.86								
D6762	37062		10.62	51L	52A	01.70	re	02.74	TE	01.82	TI	07.87	WDN	03.89		
D6763	37063		11.62	51L	52A	01.70	re	01.74	TE	05.81	ED	01.87	TI	05.87		
D6764	37064	37515	11.62	51L	52A	01.70	31B	10.72	re	02.74	HM	05.76	SF	10.76		
					TI	01.80	SF	01.82	HM	05.84	TI	09.84	TE	11.85	re	03.87
D6765	37065		11.62	51L	52A	01.70	re	02.74	TE	01.82	HM	05.83	TE	09.84		
					TI	05.87										
D6766	37066		11.62	51L	52A	01.70	re	02.74	TE	01.82	TI	05.87	IM	01.90		
D6767	37067	37703	11.62	51L	52A	04.70	TE	05.73	re	02.74	CF	08.86	re	01.87		
D6768	37068	37356	11.62	51L	52A	01.70	51L	06.72	52A	11.72	re	01.74				
		37068			TE	05.81	TI	07.87	re	06.88	re	06.89				
D6769	37069		07.62	51L	re	02.74										
D6770	37070		08.62	51L	52A	04.70	51L	11.72	re	01.74	ED	07.81	SF	01.82		
					TE	05.84	ED	10.87	IS	10.87	TE	05.89				
D6771	37071		08.62	51L	52A	04.70	re	01.74	TE	01.82	HM	10.82	TE	09.84		
					TI	05.87	IM	11.89								
D6772	37072		09.62	51L	52A	01.70	51L	11.72	re	02.74	TI	05.87	CF	05.90		
D6773	37073		09.62	51L	31B	10.71	SY	06.73	MC	07.73	re	01.74	GD	01.76		
					TE	05.81	TI	07.87								
D6774	37074		09.62	51L	31B	10.71	D16	03.73	TO	05.73	MC	06.73	re	02.74		
					TE	03.74	TI	07.81	SF	01.82	TE	05.84	SF	05.88	TI	07.89
D6775	37075		09.62	51L	50B	06.64	51L	12.67	MR	02.74	re	02.74	HM	05.84		
					TI	09.84	TE	03.86	SF	01.87	ML	10.87	SF	11.87	TE	07.89
D6776	37076	37518	10.62	51L	52A	11.72	re	10.73	TE	05.81	TE	07.81	TI	01.87		
					TE	04.87	re	06.87								
D6777	37077		10.62	51L	55C	01.70	51L	02.70	31B	10.71	52A	10.72	51L	11.72		
					re	01.74	TI	07.81	SF	01.82	HM	10.82	GD	01.83	TE	11.84
					SF	05.88	TI	07.89	ML	07.90						
D6778	37078		10.62	51L	31B	10.71	D16	01.73	31B	03.73	SY	07.73	MR	10.73		
					re	02.74	GD	01.76	TE	07.81	CF	05.88				
D6779	37079	37357	11.62	50B	51L	08.64	52A	05.69	51L	07.69	re	03.74	GD	03.74		
		37079			TE	10.75	ED	01.87	TI	05.87	re	06.88	re	03.90		
D6780	37080		11.62	50B	51L	07.63	52A	06.67	51L	09.67	40B	04.69	51L	07.69		
					re	01.74	GD	02.75	TE	10.75	HM	09.79	IM	01.80	SF	01.82
					HM	10.82	TI	09.84	MR	01.86	GD	03.86	MR	09.86	TI	05.87
					ED	07.87										
D6781	37081	37797	11.62	50B	51L	07.63	50B	06.64	41A	10.69	IM	09.73	re	02.74		
					TI	03.74	ML	01.79	ED	03.79	CF	05.86	re	05.86		
D6782	37082	37502	11.62	50B	51L	07.63	50B	06.64	41A	10.69	31B	10.72				
					TE	02.74	GD	03.74	TE	02.75	GD	05.75	TE	01.82		
					HM	10.82	GD	09.84	CF	08.85	re	03.86	TE	01.87		
D6783	37083		12.62	50B	51L	07.63	50B	06.64	41A	10.69	31B	10.72	re	03.74		
					GD	02.75	TE	01.82	HM	05.83	GD	09.84	IM	07.85	TE	05.87
D6784	37084	37718	12.62	50B	50A	07.66	HEA	01.67	50B	06.67	41A	10.69				
					52A	10.72	re	10.73	TE	02.75	MR	05.76	SF	05.86	ED	07.87
					SF	11.87	re	02.89								
D6785	37085	37711	12.62	52A	50A	07.66	50B	02.67	51L	05.67	52A	03.69				
					51L	07.69	55C	02.70	41A	10.70	D16	12.71	41A	12.71	52A	10.72
					re	03.74	TE	03.74	MR	05.76	SF	02.81	ED	02.81	su	02.88
					ED	03.88	CF	03.88	re	06.88						
D6786	37086	37516	12.62	52A	50A	07.66	50B	02.67	51L	05.67	52A	07.67				
					51L	09.67	52A	07.69	51L	01.70	41A	10.71	IM	09.73	re	02.74
					TI	03.74	SF	05.86	TE	01.87	re	04.87				
D6787	37087		12.62	52A	50A	07.66	50B	02.67	51L	05.67	52A	06.67	51L	09.67		
					52A	10.72	re	02.74	TE	02.75	TI	06.75	MR	05.76	SF	05.86
					TI	07.89	ED	03.90								
D6788	37088	37323	01.63	52A	50A	07.66	50B	02.67	41A	10.69	re	02.74				
		37088			MR	10.76	ED	05.85	ML	12.85	TI	07.86	re	09.89	ED	05.90
D6789	37089	37708	01.63	52A	50A	07.66	50B	02.67	41A	10.69	IM	09.73	re	02.74		
					TI	03.74	SF	05.77	re	02.88	IM	09.89	ED	11.89		
D6790	37090	37508	01.63	52A	50A	07.66	50B	02.67	41A	10.69	SF	09.73	MR	05.74		
					re	05.74	TI	06.75	HM	05.76	TE	10.76	MR	03.77	TE	07.83
					ED	05.84	CF	01.86	re	05.86	TI	01.87				
D6791	37091	37358	01.63	52A	50A	10.66	50B	02.67	52A	10.68	51L	01.70				
					41A	10.71	IM	09.73	re	01.74	TI	03.74	SF	05.77	MR	02.81
					IM	05.81	SF	11.81	re	03.88	TI	07.89				

1958 No.	TOPS No.	TOPS ren	Ent. Serv	1st Dep	Shed	Date Trans	Shed	Date Trans	Shed	Date Trans	Shed	Date Trans	Shed	Date Trans	Shed	Date Trans
D6792	37092		02.63	52A	50A	10.66	50B	02.67	51L	05.68	52A	10.68	52A	10.68		
					re	02.74	TI	06.75	MR	10.76	SF	05.86	ML	07.87	ED	08.87
					ML	11.87										
D6793	37093	37509	02.63	52A	50A	07.66	50B	02.67	51L	05.68	re	02.74	HM	05.76		
					TI	10.75	TE	01.80	GD	08.80	TE	01.82	GD	10.82	CF	01.86
					re	06.86	TE	01.87								
D6794	37094	37716	02.63	52A	50A	10.66	50B	02.67	51L	04.68	52A	09.68				
					51L	04.70	52A	10.72	55C	11.72	41A	12.72	55C	03.73	re	11.73
					IM	05.74	TI	10.75	HM	05.76	IM	10.78	MR	09.79	IM	01.80
					SF	01.8	IM	05.88	CF	07.88						
D6795	37095		03.63	52A	50A	07.66	50B	02.67	51L	04.68	52A	09.68	51L	11.72		
					re	02.74	TI	03.74	IM	03.74	HM	01.79	TE	11.79	GD	06.80
					TE	05.82	TI	10.87	IM	01.90						
D6796	37096		11.62	41A	41A	04.64	41C	08.67	51L	09.67	52A	12.67	55C	11.72		
					IM	09.73	re	03.74	MR	01.76	TE	03.77	MR	10.78	HM	02.79
					GD	05.80	TE	05.82	TI	05.87	Su	09.89	Su	05.90		
D6797	37097		12.62	41A	41A	04.64	52A	09.67	51L	10.67	52A	12.67	55C	05.71		
					31B	10.72	55C	03.73	IM	09.73	re	02.74	TE	08.74	MR	10.78
					TI	05.87	ML	07.87	ED	06.88	ML	05.89				
D6798	37098		12.62	41A	41A	04.64	41C	08.67	52A	09.67	51L	10.67	52A	11.67		
					55C	01.70	IM	09.73	re	03.74	HM	08.74	TE	04.79	HM	09.79
					TE	11.79	GD	09.85	TE	07.86	TI	01.87	TE	10.89		
D6799	37099	37324	12.62	41A	41A	04.64	52A	09.67	40B	08.72	55C	11.72				
		37099			MR	09.73	re	03.74	GD	03.75	MR	08.78	ED	09.81	SF	11.81
					MR	05.83	ED	05.85	ML	11.85	re	07.86	IS	05.88	ML	08.88
					re	09.89										
D6800	37100		12.62	41A	41A	04.64	re	02.74	GD	03.74	TE	10.75	GD	09.79		
					TE	11.86	TI	01.87	TE	07.87	SF	11.87	TE	07.89		
D6801	37101		12.62	41A	41A	04.64	51L	10.71	TI	01.74	re	02.74	GD	03.75		
					MR	10.75	TE	02.77	GD	09.79	TE	05.82	GD	09.85	TE	07.86
					TI	01.87										
D6802	37102	37712	01.63	41A	41A	04.64	51L	10.71	re	02.74	MR	02.74	GD	03.75		
					MH	10.75	TI	05.87	ED	07.87	CF	05.88	re	00.00		
D6803	37103	37511	01.63	41A	41A	04.64	IM	09.73	re	02.74	TI	03.74	HM	01.79		
					SF	05.80	MR	02.81	IM	05.81	SF	11.81	MR	05.84	CF	03.86
					re	07.86	TE	01.87								
D6804	37104		01.63	41A	41A	04.64	52A	01.71	TI	01.74.re		02.74	TE	10.76		
					HM	09.79	IM	09.84	SF	01.87	TI	07.89	CF	11.89	IM	12.89
D6805	37105	37796	01.63	41A	41A	04.64	IM	09.73	re	01.74	TI	03.74	HM	01.79		
					SF	01.82	HM	10.83	MR	11.83	CF	05.86	re	11.86		
D6806	37106		01.63	41A	41A	04.64	52A	10.71	re	02.74	TI	03.74	GD	03.75		
					HM	10.83	TI	09.84	IM	07.85						
D6807	37107		01.63	41A	41A	04.64	52A	10.71	re	01.74	TI	03.74	HM	05.75		
					TI	06.75	MR	10.76	ML	05.87	ED	08.87	SF	11.87	TI	07.89
D6808	37108	37325	01.63	41A	41A	04.64	re	05.74	ED	01.78	ML	05.86	re	07.86	ED	05.88
		37108			ML	06.88	re	09.89								
D6809	37109		02.63	41A	41A	04.64	51L	10.71	re	02.74	MR	02.74	TI	10.74	MR	02.75
					ML	05.87	IS	05.88	TE	05.89						
D6810	37110		02.63	41A	41A	04.64	51L	10.71	re	02.74	MR	02.74	ML	05.87	IS	05.88
					TE	04.89										
D6811	37111	37326	02.63	41A	41A	04.64	SF	09.73	re	03.74	MR	05.74	TI	10.76		
		37111			ED	01.78	ML	01.86	re	07.86	ML	07.88	re	07.89		
D6812	37112	37510	02.63	41A	41A	04.64	51L	10.71	re	02.74	MR	02.74	TI	10.76		
					HM	01.79	GD	05.80	ED	06.80	CF	02.86	re	06.86	TE	01.87
D6813	37113		02.63	41A	41A	04.64	51L	10.71	MR	02.74	re	02.74	TE	03.77		
					HM	09.79	MR	11.83	TI	05.87	ML	07.87	ED	10.87	WDN	03.89
					in	08.89	IS	09.89	ED	05.90						
D6814	37114		02.63	41A	41A	04.64	51L	10.71	MR	02.74	re	02.74	ED	01.81		
					IS	05.82	ED	05.90								
D6815	37115	37514	02.63	41A	41A	04.64	IM	09.73	TI	11.73	re	05.74	SF	02.77		
					MR	03.81	IM	05.81	SF	06.81	MR	05.83	TE	01.87	re	03.87
D6816	37116		03.63	41A	41A	04.64	31B	01.71	IM	09.73	TI	11.73	re	02.74		
					SF	02.75	TI	07.89	ML	09.90						
D6817	37117	37521	03.63	41A	41A	04.64	30A	03.68	31B	10.69	re	02.74				
					TE	02.74	ED	08.80	ML	11.82	ED	12.85	TI	05.87	IM	01.88
					CF	03.88	re	04.88								
D6818	37118	37359	03.63	41A	41A	04.64	30A	03.68	52A	02.69	51L	08.72	re	02.74	TI	03.74
					MR	05.74	TI	10.76	SF	02.77	ED	04.87	re	11.88		
D6819	37283	37895	03.63	88A	52A	07.66	30A	02.69	31B	10.72	D16	10.72				
					31B	12.72	re	02.74	TI	10.76	IM	05.77	SF	05.80	HM	01.82
					TI	09.84	CF	08.86	re	02.87						
D6820	37120	37887	03.63	88A	52A	07.66	51L	11.68	52A	01.70	30A	10.70.				
					31B	10.72	SY	10.73	MR	12.73	re	03.74	TI	05.76	SF	01.79
					TI	09.84	CF	03.85	TI	11.85	CF	07.87	SF	08.87	re	02.88
					CF	05.88										
D6821	37121	37677	04.63	88A	86A	07.64	64B	07.66	51L	09.66	HEA	02.67				
					52A	10.67	51L	09.68	41A	05.70	TE	09.73	re	02.74	TI	05.74
					TI	05.76	HM	05.79	GD	05.80	TI	01.82	GD	01.83	BR	05.83
					TI	11.84	re	05.87								

1958 No.	TOPS No.	TOPS ren	Ent. Serv	1st Dep	Shed Date Trans	Shed Date Trans	Shed Date Trans	Shed Date Trans	Shed Date Trans	Shed Date Trans
D6822	37122	37692	04.63	88A	51L 10.66	HEA 02.67	52A 10.67	51L 11.68	41A 05.70	
					TE 09.73	TI 05.74	SF 09.79	TI 01.82	TE 09.86	
					re 01.87	TI ??.??	CF 02.87			
D6823	37123	37679	04.63	88A	52A 07.66	51L 11.68	41A 05.71	re 03.74		
					BR 05.83	TI 11.84	CF 03.85	TI 11.85	re 05.87	
D6824	37124	37894	04.63	88A	52A 07.66	51L 10.68	41A 05.70	re 04.74		
					IM 01.79	MR 09.79	IM 01.80	LE 04.82	ED 09.82	LE 03.85
					TI 11.85	CF 08.86	re 01.87			
D6825	37125	37904	05.63	88A	52A 07.66	30A 10.68	31B 10.72	SF 09.73	re 03.74	
					TI 03.75	IM 01.79	MR 09.79	IM 01.80	ML 03.81	SF 05.85
					MR 06.85	ML 08.85	ED 12.85	GD 03.86	TI 07.86	CF 08.86
					re 04.87					
D6826	37126	37676	05.63	88A	52A 07.66	51L 05.69	41A 05.70	re 05.74	IM 01.79	
					MR 09.79	IM 01.80	HM 01.82	TI 09.84	CF 03.85	TI 11.85
					re 05.87					
D6827	37127	37370	05.63	88A	52A 07.66	41A 05.71	TI 03.74.	SY 02.74	re 05.74	
					IM 01.79	CF 04.81	BR 07.81	GD 11.82	BR 05.83	SF 03.86
					CF 01.87	IM 10.87	ML 05.88	re 07.88		
D6828	37128		06.63	88A	52A 07.66	51L 01.70	41A 05.70	51L 01.71	52A 02.71	
					30A 10.71	re 04.74	IM 01.79	CF 04.81	BR 07.81	GD 11.82
					TI 09.86	CF 07.87	TE 10.87	SF 11.87	TI 07.89	
					IS 11.89	ED 05.90				
D6829	37129	37669	03.63	88A	51L 10.66	HEA 01.67	HEA 02.67	52A 12.67		
					51L 12.68	41A 05.70	51L 01.71	52A 02.71	30A 10.71	37129 03.74
					ML 01.79	LE 04.82	CF 05.82	BR 01.83	IS 07.86	TI 12.86
					ED 08.87	re 08.87	LA 01.88			
D6830	37130	37681	03.63	88A	52A 07.66	51L 07.69	41A 05.70	51L 01.71		
					52A 02.71	30A 03.71	re 03.74	MR 11.81	TI 01.82	IM 01.83
					TI 01.85	re 04.87				
D6831	37131		03.63	88A	87E 06.63	50A 09.66	52A 10.66	51L 09.68	30A 10.68	
					re 03.74	TE 02.76	CF 10.76	TI 02.77	IM 01.79	HM 01.82
					CF 05.84	TI 11.84	CF 01.87			
D6832	37132	37673	04.63	88A	50A 09.66	52A 10.66	HEA 02.67	52A 11.67		
					51L 03.69	52A 07.69	51L 01.70	30A 06.71	re 02.74	TI 06.75
					IM 01.79	TI 01.82	GD 01.84	IM 06.85	SF 01.87	LA 04.87
					re 07.87					
D6833	37133		04.63	88A	50A 09.66	52A 10.66	HEA 02.67	52A 11.67	30A 10.71	
					TI 05.73	7re 05.74	ML 12.79	ED 12.85	GD 03.86	ED 03.86
					ML 05.87	CF 07.87				
D6834	37134	37684	04.63	88A	50A 10.66	HEA 01.67	52A 11.67	51L 03.69		
					41A 05.71	re 02.74	CF 04.81	BR 07.81	GD 11.82	IM 06.85
					SF 07.86	TE 11.86	TI 01.87	re 03.87		
D6835	37135	37888	04.63	88A	50A 10.66	50B 11.66	55C 10.69	41A 07.70		
					D16 10.71	41A 12.71	TO 02.74	TI 03.74	re 05.74	SF 04.81
					BR 07.81	TE 03.87	CF 07.87	SF 08.87	re 12.87	IM 04.90
D6836	37136	37905	04.63	88A	87E 06.63	50A 10.66	50B 11.66	55C 10.69	re 02.74	
					GD 01.83	CF 05.86	re 11.86			
D6837	37137	37312 37137	04.63	88A	64B 09.66	66A 09.67	51L 11.68	64B 02.71		
					66A 03.71	86A 01.72	LE 11.73	re 04.74	IM 08.74	TI 06.75
					MR 09.78	ED 01.79	ML 12.79	SF 07.86	re 02.89	
D6838	37138		04.63	88A	64B 09.63	66A 09.66	65A 09.68	re 03.74	ED 01.79	LE 10.79
					BR 05.80	CD 07.80	CF 05.81	GD 11.82	MR 05.85	SF 06.85
					MR 09.85	SF 05.87	IM 11.89	CF 03.90		
D6839	37139		05.63	88A	66A 08.66	65A 03.72	86A 06.72	LE 11.73.	TI 01.74	
					re 05.74	MR 09.78	TI 12.78	CF 10.85	TE 05.86	MR 09.86
					CF 01.87					
D6840	37140		05.63	88A	66A 08.66	65A 12.66	66A 08.67	64B 02.71	66A 03.71	65A 03.72
					64B 10.72	65A 11.72	LE 11.73	re 12.73	TI 02.74	TO 02.74
					TI 03.74	IM 11.77	ML 12.79	SF 03.81	MR 11.81	SF 05.87
D6841	37141		05.63	88A	66A 08.66	64B 02.71	66A 03.71	65A 03.72	86A 11.72	
					LE 11.73	re 06.74	IM 08.74	TI 06.75	TO 02.78	HM 09.79
					TE 05.80	SF 07.81	IM 11.81	SF 05.84	ED 05.87	CF 07.87
D6842	37142		05.63	88A	66A 08.66	65A 03.72	87A 11.72	re 03.74	LA 02.78	
					CF 04.83	TE 03.86	MR 09.86	TI 05.87	CF 07.87	BR 10.87
					CF 05.88					
D6843	37143	37800	05.63	88A	66A 08.66	65A 09.68	re 05.74	CF 11.74	TI 02.77	
					IM 11.77	SF 05.84	CF 03.86	re 09.86		
D6844	37144		06.63	88A	64B 09.66	65A 09.68	re 03.74	MR 05.85	SF 05.87	
D6845	37145	37313 37145	06.63	88A	64B 09.66	65A 09.68	re 03.74	ML 02.80		
					IS 05.86	ML 06.86	re 08.86	re 09.89		
D6846	37146		06.63	88A	64B 09.66	65A 11.72	re 01.74	ML 11.79	ED 11.82	
					ML 06.83	IS 05.86	ED 11.86	CF 07.87	BR 10.87	TE 01.88
					CF 05.88					
D6847	37147	37371	06.63	88A	64B 09.66	65A 10.78	re 09.74	IM 03.85	LE ??.??	CF 01.87
					IM 11.87	CF 05.88	re 10.88			
D6848	37148	37800	06.63	88A	64B 09.66	65A 09.68	re 03.74	ML 04.80	ED 10.81	
					LE 04.82	BR 05.82	ED 10.82	ML 03.85	MR 05.85	CF 03.86
					re 10.86					
D6849	37149	37892	06.63	88A	64B 09.66	65A 09.68	re 09.74	LE 03.85	CF 01.87	
					SF 08.87	re 10.87	IM 04.90			
D6850	37150	37901	07.63	88A	64B 09.66	65A 05.70	re 04.74	ML 11.79	ED 01.84	
					ML 01.84	CF 03.85	SF 11.85	CF 02.86	re 10.86	

1958 No.	TOPS No.	TOPS ren	Ent. Serv	1st Dep	Shed	Date Trans	Shed	Date Trans	Shed	Date Trans	Shed	Date Trans	Shed	Date Trans	Shed	Date Trans
D6851	37151	37667	07.63	88A	64B	09.66	65A	10.70	re	05.74	BR	04.82	ED	10.82		
					ML	10.84	ED	12.85	TE	03.88	re	06.88				
D6852	37152	37310	07.63	87E	86A	11.64	87E	04.66	66A	08.66	65A	03.72				
		37152			re	09.74	ML	04.80	IM	07.81	ED	01.84	re	03.86	ML	??.??
					re	09.89	ML	??.??	ED	05.90						
D6853	37153		07.63	87E	66A	08.66	64B	01.71	66A	04.71	65A	03.72	re	04.74		
					IM	07.81	IS	07.88	ED	05.89						
D6854	37154		07.63	87E	66A	08.66	64B	01.71	66A	04.71	65A	03.72	re	09.74		
					ML	03.79	CF	11.84	IM	05.86	SF	05.88	TI	07.89	IS	11.89
					ED	05.90										
D6855	37155	37897	07.63	87E	86A	11.64	87E	04.66	66A	08.66	64B	01.71				
					66A	02.72	65A	03.72	re	04.74	ML	04.82	IM	06.85	ML	07.85
					IS	05.86	CF	07.86	re	12.86						
D6856	37156	37311	07.63	87E	66A	08.66	65A	03.72	re	05.74	ML	02.79				
		37156			re	03.86	re	09.89	ED	02.90						
D6857	37157	37695	07.63	87E	66A	08.66	64B	10.66	65A	10.69	re	03.74	ML	02.79		
					CF	02.86	re	06.86								
D6858	37158		08.63	87E	64B	09.66	65A	11.72	87A	11.72	re	03.74	BR	05.80	MR	05.86
					CF	01.87	BR	10.87	CF	05.88						
D6859	37159	37372	06.63	88A	86A	04.66	66A	08.66	64B	10.66	66A	09.67	65A	03.72		
					87A	11.72	re	03.74	BR	05.80	SF	05.86	CF	01.87	re	06.88
D6860	37160	37373	07.63	88A	87E	04.66	86A	09.66	HEA	11.66	41A	07.70	52A	01.71		
					30A	10.71	51L	03.73	re	02.74	SF	??.??	ML	05.87	ED	10.87
					re	07.88										
D6861	37161	37899	07.63	87E	86A	09.66	41A	07.70	TE	09.73	re	03.74	SF	10.75		
					TI	02.76	IM	06.77	SF	01.85	IM	??.??	CF	06.86	re	12.86
					TI	05.87	ED	10.87	ML	05.88						
D6862	37162		07.63	87E	86A	09.66	HEA	11.66	41A	08.72	MR	09.73	CF	01.74		
					re	04.74	HM	09.79	TE	11.79	IM	05.82	BR	07.86	CF	08.87
D6863	37163	37802	08.63	87E	41A	07.70	TE	09.73	re	01.74	re	05.86				
D6864	37164	37675	08.63	87E	41A	07.70	IM	07.73	re	02.74	TE	03.74	CF	05.83		
					LA	04.87	re	05.87								
D6865	37165	37374	08.63	87E	HEA	11.66	31B	06.69	30A	10.69	40B	03.73				
		37165			re	02.74	TE	03.74	HM	10.82	TI	09.4	CF	11.84	re	??.??
					ED	01.89	re	07.89								
D6866	37166	37891	09.63	86A	51L	06.69	30A	03.70	51L	04.70	30A	02.72	40B	03.73		
					re	02.74	TE	05.75	SF	07.81	IM	11.81	SF	05.84	CF	01.87
					SF	03.87	re	09.87	IM	04.90						
D6867	37167		09.63	86A	41A	07.70	TE	09.73	re	02.74	CF	11.84	BR	08.86	CF	08.87
D6868	37168	37890	10.63	86A	41A	07.70	TE	09.73	re	01.74	TI	03.75	IM	11.77		
					SF	05.84	re	11.87	IM	04.90						
D6869	37169	37674	08.63	87E	41A	07.70	LA	04.87	re	05.87						
D6870	37170		08.63	87E	41A	10.71	re	05.74	IM	10.77	MR	01.80	HM	05.83	TI	09.84
					ML	05.87	ED	08.87	ML	08.87	ED	10.87				
D6871	37171		09.63	86A	52A	05.68	51L	05.69	52A	07.69	51L	01.70	40B	08.72		
					re	03.74	MR	01.80	ED	09.82	CF	07.85	MR	03.86	TI	05.86
					TE	11.86	TE	01.87	CF	02.87	re	02.87				
D6872	37172	37686	09.63	86A	52A	05.68	51L	03.69	40B	08.72	re	02.74				
					MR	01.80	ED	09.82	CF	03.85	ED	08.86	TE	11.86	TI	01.87
					re	02.87										
D6873	37173	37801	09.63	87E	51L	12.72	re	02.74	MR	01.80	CF	04.86	re	09.86		
D6874	37174		09.63	86A	51L	04.69	52A	07.69	51L	01.70	40B	10.72	re	02.74		
					MR	01.80	SF	12.80	TI	01.82	MR	01.86	CF	01.87	TI	03.87
					CF	07.87	BR	10.87	CF	05.88						
D6875	37175		09.63	86A	re	03.74	ED	10.82	LA	05.86	IS	10.87	ED	05.89		
D6876	37176	37883	10.63	86A	re	04.74	BR	10.82	CF	05.85	BR	05.86	TE	05.86		
					TI	09.86	TE	07.87	SF	11.87	CF	05.88	re	12.88		
D6877	37177	37885	10.63	86A	87E	04.66	re	03.74	CF	01.87	TE	03.87	SF	11.87		
					CF	05.88	re	10.88								
D6878	37178		10.63	86A	M16	06.65	86A	10.65	87A	10.71	re	05.74	CF	12.75		
					ED	10.82	SF	11.87	TI	05.89						
D6879	37179	37691	10.63	86A	87A	10.71	re	12.73	ED	04.82	CF	03.85	TI	11.85		
					GD	03.86	TE	11.86	TI	01.87	CF	02.87	re	02.87		
D6880	37180	37886	10.63	87E	re	11.73	CF	01.87	GD	03.87	TE	07.87	CF	05.88	re	??.??
D6881	37181	37687	10.63	86A	87E	04.66	re	02.74	LA	10.82	CF	08.85	TE	11.86	GD	02.87
					re	03.87										
D6882	37182	37670	10.63	86A	87E	04.66	re	03.74	LA	10.82	CF	04.83	LA	12.83		
					CF	05.84	BR	05.85	GD	02.87	LA	04.88	re	08.87		
D6883	37183	37884	11.63	87E	re	03.74	ED	04.82	IS	04.82	ED	01.86	ML	05.87		
					CF	06.88	ML	06.88	re	11.88						
D6884	37184		11.63	87E	re	02.74	ED	04.82	IS	09.82	ED	10.82	ML	12.85	IS	05.86
					ED	11.86	IM	11.89								
D6885	37185		12.63	87E	86A	11.64	87E	10.65	86A	04.66	re	03.74	LA	04.83		
					CF	02.85	BR	05.85	TE	05.86	ED	10.86	TE	11.86	ED	11.86
D6886	37186	37889	11.63	87E	86A	04.66	re	05.74	re	12.86						
					TE	05.87										
D6887	37187	37683	01.64	87E	re	02.74	BR	11.81	CF	05.85	TE	11.86	TI	01.87	re	03.87
D6888	37188		01.64	87E	re	04.74	BR	11.81	ED	04.82	ML	12.85	ED	01.86		
D6889	37189	37672	01.64	86A	87E	10.65	re	04.74	BR	11.81	CF	05.85	BR	03.86		
					LA	04.87	re	07.87								
D6890	37190	37314	01.64	87E	re	02.74	ED	??.??	ML	11.85	re	07.86				
D6891	37191		02.64	87E	86A	04.64	87E	04.66	re	02.74	TI	11.81				

1958 No.	TOPS No.	TOPS ren	Ent. Serv	1st Dep	Shed	Date Trans	Shed	Date Trans	Shed	Date Trans	Shed	Date Trans	Shed	Date Trans	Shed	Date Trans
D6892	**37192**	**37694**	02.64	87E	86A	11.64	87E	04.66	re	03.74	ED	11.81	CF	03.85	ML	12.85
					CF	01.86	ML	01.86	CF	??.??	re	06.86	ED	09.89		
D6893	**37193**	**37375**	02.64	87E	86A	06.66	87E	12.66	51L	01.70	re	03.74	BR	03.87		
					CF	08.87	re	??.??	ED	01.89						
D6894	**37194**		03.64	87E	86A	06.66	87E	12.66	52A	03.67	51L	01.70	re	03.74		
					TI	07.87										
D6895	**37195**	**37689**	03.64	87E	86A	06.66	87E	12.66	52A	03.67	51L	01.70	re	02.74		
D6896	**37196**		04.64	87E	86A	06.66	87E	12.66	52A	03.67	51L	04.70	86A	01.72		
					LE	11.73	re	04.74	ED	07.80	CF	11.84	LA	02.85	??	07.85
					CF	07.87	IS	10.87	ED	05.89						
D6897	**37197**		04.64	87E	86A	06.66	52A	03.67	51L	01.70	re	02.74	CF	11.84		
D6898	**37198**		05.64	87E	86A	07.64	52A	03.67	51L	01.70	re	02.74	TI	07.87		
D6899	**37199**	**37376**	10.63	86A	52A	03.67	51L	01.70	55C	01.72	re	02.74	TE	05.75		
					GD	10.75	BR	02.87	CF	08.87	re	06.88	ED	01.89		
D6900	**37200**	**37377**	10.63	86A	52A	03.67	TE	09.73	re	01.74	CF	03.87	re	05.88		
					IM	07.88										
D6901	**37201**		10.63	86A	52A	03.67	51L	11.70	55C	01.72	40B	08.72	re	10.73		
					ML	07.88										
D6902	**37202**		10.63	86A	52A	03.67	51L	01.70	55C	01.72	40B	08.72	re	01.74		
					TE	05.89										
D6903	**37203**		10.63	86A	64B	04.67	66A	01.71	64B	02.72	86A	06.72	LE	11.73		
					re	05.74	BR	07.79	IM	03.86	SF	05.88	IM	10.88	TE	05.89
D6904	**37204**	**37378**	11.63	86A	65A	05.68	66A	09.68	65A	03.72	re	04.74				
					TI	01.78	CF	09.78	ED	05.79	CF	un	BR	07.79	TE	08.87
					TI	10.8	re	06.88	TE	04.90						
D6905	**37205**	**37688**	11.63	87E	86A	09.67	65A	05.68	66A	11.68	65A	03.72.	re	05.74		
					TI	01.78	CF	09.78	BR	07.79	CF	03.81	LE	10.82	TE	10.86
					CF	??.??	TI	02.87	re	02.87						
D6906	**37206**	**37906**	11.63	87E	86A	11.64	87E	02.65	86A	09.67	87A	06.72	re	06.74		
					CF	04.83	BR	05.05	CF	06.86	re	12.86				
D6907	**37207**		11.63	87E	86A	09.67	87A	06.72	re	05.74	BR	08.79	LA	??.??	BR	10.87
					CF	05.88										
D6908	**37208**	**37803**	11.63	87E	86A	03.67	87A	06.72	re	02.74	BR	??.??	CF	06.86	re	05.86
D6909	**37209**		12.63	87E	86A	09.67	87A	06.72	re	12.73	TI	02.74	BR	08.79	TI	??.??
					SF	11.87	TI	07.89	ML	09.90						
D6910	**37210**	**37693**	11.63	87E	86C	01.69	87A	06.72	re	02.74	BR	09.79	CF	03.81		
					re	07.86	TE	??.??	TI	01.87	CF	03.87	ED	02.90		
D6911	**37211**		12.63	87E	52A	10.68	52A	11.69	51L	01.70	55C	01.72	40B	08.72		
					re	01.74	SF	01.87	CF	09.88	SF	01.89	CF	05.89	SF	07.89
D6912	**37212**		01.64	87E	86C	01.69	41A	04.69	52A	07.69	TE	09.73	re	02.74		
					GD	09.79	CF	01.87	SF	01.89						
D6913	**37213**		01.64	87E	86A	11.64	87E	02.65	86A	03.65	41A	04.69	52A	07.69		
					51L	04.70	52A	10.70	86A	01.72	re	03.74				
D6914	**37214**		01.64	86A	87E	02.65	HEA	09.67	86A	05.71	re	04.74	LE	08.86		
					CF	01.87										
D6915	**37215**		01.64	87E	HEA	10.67	41A	10.71	SF	09.73	re	03.74	TI	01.82		
					IM	11.87	SF	01.88	CF	05.88						
D6916	**37216**		01.64	87E	86A	08.64	87E	02.65	HEA	10.67	30A	09.71	51L	03.73		
					re	03.74	GD	10.75	MR	10.85	SF	05.87				
D6917	**37217**		01.64	87E	86A	07.64	87E	02.65	HEA	10.67	52A	01.70	86A	05.71		
					re	04.74										
D6918	**37218**		01.64	87E	HEA	10.67	86A	05.71	re	04.74	IM	03.86	SF	01.87		
					CF	09.88	SF	02.89								
D6919	**37219**		01.64	86A	87E	02.64	65A	05.68	64B	09.68	66A	01.71	64B	04.71		
					65A	11.72	TE	10.73	re	02.74	MR	01.80	SF	05.87		
D6920	**37220**		01.64	86A	HEA	09.67	41A	01.70	51L	05.71	re	01.74	CF	02.74		
D6921	**37221**		01.64	86A	86A	05.67	re	02.74	IM	08.74	SF	01.87	CF	10.88		
D6922	**37222**		01.64	87E	86A	03.65	HEA	09.67	86A	01.72	re	05.74	LA	08.85		
					CF	02.86	ED	09.90								
D6923	**37223**		02.64	87E	HEA	10.67	86A	05.71	re	03.74						
D6924	**37224**	**37680**	01.64	87E	86A	11.66	87E	06.67	86C	01.69	87A	10.70	re	05.74		
					BR	09.79	LE	10.82	CF	??.??	TI	02.87	re	04.87		
D6925	**37225**		02.64	87E	86A	11.66	87E	06.67	HEA	09.67	86A	01.72	re	05.74		
					LA	08.85	CF	02.86	IM	06.86						
D6926	**37226**		02.64	87E	86A	11.64	HEA	10.67	41A	10.71	re	05.74	CF	07.86		
					BR	01.88	ML	05.88								
D6927	**37227**	**37379**	02.64	87E	86A	11.64	HEA	10.67	86A	05.71	re	06.74	BR	01.88		
					ML	05.88	re	07.88	TE	01.89						
D6928	**37228**	**37376**	02.64	87E	HEA	10.67	52A	01.70	re	01.74	CF	02.74	TE	07.83	CF	??.??
					re	06.86	ED	09.88								
D6929	**37229**		02.64	87E	86A	05.71	re	03.74	ED	09.88						
D6930	**37230**		03.64	87E	86A	11.64	87E	05.67	56B	11.67	86A	05.71	re	04.74		
D6931	**37231**	**37896**	03.64	87E	re	05.74	BR	09.79	CF	02.80	BR	05.80	re	12.86		
D6932	**37232**		03.64	87E	re	03.74	BR	09.79	CF	08.87	BR	10.87	CF	05.88	ED	07.88
					IM	11.89										
D6933	**37233**	**37889**	04.64	87E	re	04.74	BR	05.80	re	11.87	SF	07.87	CF	05.88		
D6934	**37234**	**37685**	04.64	87E	re	03.74	CF	07.80	TE	11.86	TI	01.87	CF	03.87		
D6935	**37235**		04.64	87E	86A	07.64	87E	03.67	41A	04.69	52A	07.69	55C	01.70		
					52A	10.72	re	02.74	LE	08.74	CF	07.80	LA	02.86	CF	07.87
D6936	**37236**	**37682**	04.64	87E	86A	07.64	64B	09.68	65A	10.70	87A	11.72				
					re	03.74	CF	04.83	TE	11.86	CF	??.??	TI	02.87	re	03.87

1958 No.	TOPS No.	TOPS ren	Ent. Serv	1st Dep	Shed	Trans	Shed	Trans	Shed	Trans	Shed	Trans	Shed	Trans	Shed	Trans
D6937	37237	37893	05.64	86A	64B	06.68	66A	01.71	64B	04.71	65A	11.72	re	09.74		
					CF	03.85	LE	??.??	CF	01.87	SF	05.87	re	10.87	IM	04.90
D6938	37238		05.64	82A	86A	08.64	40B	05.69	30A	07.69	31B	10.69	55C	07.71		
					52A	10.72	re	02.74	TE	05.74	CF	10.76	HM	07.80	HM	06.81
					IM	09.84	SF	01.87	TI	07.89						
D6939	37239		08.64	86A	56B	12.67	86A	05.71	re	05.74						
D6940	37240		08.64	86A	56B	12.67	re	02.74	LE	08.74	CF	04.83	ED	09.88		
					TE	01.89	ED	01.90								
D6941	37241		09.64	86A	87E	01.69	86A	10.69	87A	10.70	re	04.74	BR	05.80		
					TI	08.86	CF	01.87	TI	08.87	IM	10.87	SF	01.88	IM	10.88
					TE	05.89										
D6942	37242		09.64	86A	HEA	09.67	TI	01.74	GD	02.74	re	02.74	TE	05.74		
					GD	10.75	TI	07.87								
D6943	37243	37697	09.64	86A	87E	01.69	86A	10.69	87A	10.70	CF	11.73	re	04.74		
					re	05.86										
D6944	37244		09.64	86A	87E	01.69	CF	11.73	re	02.74.						
D6945	37245		09.64	86A	HEA	08.67	52A	08.67	56B	12.67	re	03.74	TE	09.79		
					HM	11.79	SF	05.80	TI	01.82	IS	01.87	u	04.87	IS	05.87
					ED	07.87	ML	08.87	ED	06.88						
D6946	37246	37698	10.64	86A	HEA	08.67	re	03.74	TE	09.79	HM	11.79	SF	05.80		
					TI	01.82	CF	07.85	re	02.86						
D6947	37247	37671	10.64	86A	HEA	08.67	30A	02.68	re	03.74	CF	02.77	LA	05.84		
					ED	05.86	LA	04.87	re	07.87						
D6948	37248		10.64	86A	HEA	08.67	86A	01.72	re	04.74.						
D6949	37249	37903	12.64	86A	HEA	08.67	re	02.74	GD	03.75	TE	10.75	HM	10.76		
					TI	09.84	CF	07.86	re	02.87						
D6950	37250		12.64	86A	HEA	08.67	MR	09.73	TI	01.74	MR	01.74	re	01.74		
					TE	03.74	GD	??.??	CF	02.87	ED	09.88	TE	01.89		
D6951	37251		12.64	86A	HEA	08.67	51L	10.68	52A	11.69	55C	10.72	re	03.74		
					CF	10.76	IS	10.87	TI	11.87	IM	12.89				
D6952	37252		01.65	86A	HEA	08.67	51L	10.68	52A	11.69	55C	10.72	re	01.74		
					TI	09.85	GD	03.86	TI	11.86	TE	10.87	SF	11.87	TI	07.89
D6953	37253	37699	01.65	86A	HEA	08.67	41A	10.68	55C	01.70	TI	07.73	SF	09.73		
					T1	11.73	re	03.74	CF	08.74	ED	07.80	CF	03.85	re	12.85
D6954	37254		01.65	86A	87A	01.72	CF	11.73	re	04.74	??	01.85				
D6955	37255		01.65	86A	87A	01.72	CF	11.73	re	04.74	IM	06.88	TE	05.89		
D6956	37256	37678	01.65	86A	87A	01.72	CF	11.73	re	04.74	BR	01.83	TI	02.87	re	05.87
D6957	37257	37668	01.65	86A	87A	01.72	CF	11.73	re	04.74	re	05.88	TE	05.88		
D6958	37258		01.65	86A	87A	01.72	re	02.74	CF	09.86	IM	06.88	TE	05.89		
D6959	37259	37380	01.65	41A	41C	06.65	41A	05.68	SF	09.73	re	03.74				
					MR	11.81	HM	05.83	CF	05.84	TE	11.84	CF	07.87	TI	08.87
					re	06.88	ED	03.89								
D6960	37260		01.65	41A	41C	06.65	30A	07.67	41A	05.71	30A	10.71	re	12.73		
					ED	04.82	IS	05.82	WDN	08.89						
D6961	37261		01.65	41A	41C	06.65	30A	09.67	re	11.73	ED	04.82	IS	05.82	ED	05.90
D6962	37262		01.65	41A	41C	06.65	30A	09.67	30A	12.67	31B	05.68	re	02.74		
					ED	09.81	IS	05.82	ED	05.90						
D6963	37263		01.65	41A	41C	06.65	30A	10.67	re	03.74	HM	05.83	ED	05.85		
					IS	09.85	ED	01.86	ML	08.87	CF	05.88.				
D6964	37264		01.65	41A	41C	06.65	30A	10.67	31B	10.69	30A	12.69	re	01.74.		
					LE	11.81	ED	10.82	IS	10.84	ED	01.86	ML	08.87	CF	05.88
D6965	37265	37430	02.65	41A	41C	06.65	41C	04.66	30A	11.67	31B	01.69				
					30A	12.69	re	03.74	LE	11.81	ED	10.82	AB	11.82	IS	02.83
					ML	05.85	ED	01.86	re	03.86	IM	11.89				
D6966	37266	37422	02.65	41A	41C	04.66	30A	12.67	re	03.74.						
					LE	11.81	ED	03.85	ML	05.85	ED	06.85	re	01.86	CF	01.89
D6967	37267	37421	02.65	41A	41C	04.66	30A	12.67	DCD	02.68	30A	05.68	re	05.74		
					LA	02.78	LE	01.80	ED	03.85	ML	05.85	ED	06.85	re	12.85
					IS	01.86	TI	05.89	IS							
D6968	37268	37401	02.65	41A	41C	04.66	30A	11.67	DCD	02.68	30A	05.68				
					re	02.74	CF	02.77	ED	07.84	re	06.85.				
D6969	37269	37417	02.65	86A	87A	01.72	CF	11.73	re	03.74	ED	01.84	ED	01.85	re	11.85	IS	01.86
					TE	05.90										
D6970	37270	37409	03.65	86A	87A	06.72	re	02.74	CF	02.77	LA	04.83	CF	01.84		
					ED	01.85	re	09.85								
D6971	37271	37418	03.65	86E	re	03.74	CF	02.77	ED	03.85	re	11.85	IS	01.86		
D6972	37272	37431	03.65	86A	re	03.74	CF	12.83	LA	04.83	ED	01.85	ML	07.85		
					CF	01.86	re	04.86								
D6973	37273	37410	04.65	86A	re	03.74	ED	01.85	re	09.85.						
D6974	37274	37402	04.65	86A	TE	02.74	CF	04.83	ED	10.84	re	07.85.				
D6975	37275		04.65	86A	re	02.74	IM	07.88								
D6976	37276		04.65	86A	re	03.74	ED	01.85	re	10.85						
D6977	37277	37415	04.65	86A	re	05.74	IS	05.74	ED	01.85	re	11.85	IS	01.86	TE	05.90
D6978	37278		04.65	86A	re	03.74	ML	09.90								
D6979	37279	37424	05.65	86A	re	04.74	IS	01.85	ML	05.85	ED	07.85	re	01.86		
D6980	37280		05.65	86A	re	02.74										
D6981	37281	37428	05.65	86A	re	01.85	ML	05.85	CF	01.86	re	02.86				
D6982	37282	37405	05.65	86A	re	03.74	ED	11.84	re	09.85						
D6983			05.65	86A	WDN	08.66										
D6984	37284	37381	05.65	86A	re	05.74	re	06.88	IM	07.88						
D6985	37285		05.65	86A	re	03.74	IS	10.87	TI	11.87	ML	09.90				

1958 No.	TOPS No.	TOPS ren	Ent. Serv	1st Dep	Shed Trans	Date Trans	Shed Trans	Date Trans	Shed Trans	Date Trans	Shed Trans	Date Trans	Shed Trans	Date Trans	Shed Trans	Date Trans
D6986	37286	37404	06.65	86A	re	03.74	ED	10.84	re	06.85						
D6987	37287	37414	06.65	41A	86A	06.65	re	05.74	IS	01.85	ML	05.85	ED	06.85		
					re	11.85	IS	01.86	LA	05.89						
D6988	37288	37427	06.65	86A	re	03.74	ED	03.85	ML	07.85	CF	01.86	re	02.86		
D6989	37289	37408	06.65	86A	re	02.74	CF	10.78	LE	10.79	CF	07.81				
					ED	01.85	re	08.85	CF	01.89	IM	11.89				
D6990	37290	37411	06.65	86A	re	03.74	LE	12.75	CF	10.78	LE	10.79	CF	07.81		
					ED	01.85	re	11.85	CF	01.89	TI	02.89				
D6991	37291	37419	06.65	86A	re	03.74	ED	03.85	re	12.85	IS	01.86				
D6992	37292	37425	07.65	86A	re	02.74	ED	05.81	ML	10.81	ED	02.86	re	01.86		
					CF	01.89	TI	03.89								
D6993	37293		07.65	86A	re	02.74										
D6994	37294		07.65	86A	re	11.73	LE	05.80	CF	07.81						
D6995	37295	37406	07.65	86A	re	05.74	LE	10.77	BR	07.80	CF	01.84	ED	11.84		
					re	10.85										
D6996	37296	37423	07.65	86A	re	01.74	LE	10.77	CF	01.84	ED	01.85	re	01.86		
D6997	37297	37420	07.65	86A	re	03.74	LE	10.77	CF	01.83	ED	01.85	re	12.85	IS	01.86
					TE	05.90										
D6998	37298		08.65	86A	re	05.74	LE	02.77	CF	01.83	TI	10.87				
D6999	37299	37426	08.65	86A	re	02.74	LE	02.77	LA	01.80	LE	10.82	BR	01.83		
					ED	01.85	LE	02.85	ED	03.85	CF	01.86	re	02.86	IM	11.89

Above:
Trip working for No 37107 on 22 August 1984, as it leaves Buxton South Junction for Briggs Sidings. *Steve Turner*